I0820427

GREENS

&

GRAINS

GREENS & GRAINS

Plant-based recipes with grains, seeds and vegetables

Anne-Katrin Weber
Photography by Wolfgang Schardt

GRUB STREET • LONDON

CONTENTS

RECIPES

FOREWORD

OF ANCIENT WHEAT, TRENDY GRAINS, AND PLENTY OF VEGETABLES

Greens & Grains – the following pages are all about vegetables, grains, and grain-like foods. However it's not just about all kinds of vegetables and the familiar types of grains, but also about the so-called pseudo-cereals, which are sometimes referred to as grain-like foods. What distinguishes 'true' grains from 'pseudo-cereals' is something you can read about in the following pages. Because this book aims to offer you more than just recipes – although I do, of course, wholeheartedly recommend all the recipes to you!

Alongside the classic, common grain varieties like wheat, spelt, oats, rye, barley, and corn, I also focus on many other *grains*. For example, the so-called ancient grains – varieties like emmer, einkorn, and kamut, which have been increasingly cultivated again in organic agriculture in recent years. Rice plays a major role worldwide, and thus also in this book – whether round or long, white, brown, or red. It's also about buckwheat, millet, quinoa, amaranth, and other seeds.

Of course, it's also about vegetables. That's already in the title – *greens* – but also in (almost) every recipe! Vegetables have been one of my favourite foods not just since *Greens & Beans*. My love of vegetables runs like a red (or better yet: green) thread through my kitchen, my recipes, my cookbooks, and naturally also through our garden, the lawn area of which is steadily shrinking while the vegetable beds are spreading. But let me reassure you: The fluffy brioche burger buns, the creamy porridge for breakfast, or the crispy granola bars come entirely without celery, spinach, or salsify.

I've created recipes for you with whole grains, with flakes, cracked grain, semolina, and flour. All the recipes – whether salad or soup, pasta, skillet or oven dishes, cake or cookies, sweet or snack – are vegetarian or vegan. Many are kept simple and use ingredients that you probably already have in your kitchen or can get anywhere, so you can start cooking or baking right away. They're all delicious. Try them out – and feel free to let me know if my promise holds true.

I wish you lots of joy with *Greens & Grains*.

Warmly,
Anne-Katrin

OATMEAL
MILLET
AMARANTH
OATS
TRICOLOUR QUINOA
BUCKWHEAT FLOUR
WHITE QUINOA
BUCKWHEAT

RYE
CRACKED RYE
POLENTA
PEARL BARLEY
BARLEY

GREENS – FROM ARTICHOKE TO ONION

Vegetables, greens, are my favourite – whether on the plate or in the garden. Under greens I include all vegetables, mushrooms, herbs, and wild herbs. For me, hardly a meal goes by without salad or spinach, sweet potatoes or celery. And when a recipe doesn't actually call for vegetables, I simply add them in, top it with fresh herbs, or prepare a bowl of salad alongside.

SEASONAL VEGETABLES

I'm always amazed at how little people know about when which vegetables grow, when they ripen, and when they are harvested. Sure, carrots, celery, and beetroot are available all year round thanks to good storage options, but even these robust, always-available vegetables have their own season. Try biting into a freshly harvested carrot in late spring – it's so sweet and aromatic, no well-stored carrot can compare.

SPRINGTIME JOY: ASPARAGUS AND YOUNG VEGETABLES

Let's not even talk about 'real' seasonal vegetables! The most famous seasonal vegetable, asparagus, has a clearly defined end: June 24th. However, many don't realise that the start of the asparagus season has been moving earlier in the calendar year. Thanks to the use of plastic sheeting under which the heat-loving stalks grow, the first asparagus can now be harvested as early as mid-March. From an ecological point of view, I view this development critically, and so I'm happy to wait each year for my first asparagus in late May.

But waiting for the fine spears rewards me twice over: the anticipation is great, the enjoyment of asparagus even greater! And saying goodbye isn't hard, since by the end of June many other vegetables are ripe and I can harvest abundantly. I've already pulled the first radishes from the soil and am thrilled about lettuce, kohlrabi, peas, and sugar snap peas, which I can pick fresh from the garden every day.

VEGETABLES IN SUMMER, AUTUMN, AND WINTER

The transition to summer vegetables is seamless. Then I indulge especially in fruiting vegetables – aubergines, peppers, tomatoes, and courgettes – my kitchen takes on a more Mediterranean flair, and the scent of garlic seems to linger constantly in the air. At the weekly market I marvel at the abundance on display: beetroot with fresh greens, juicy cucumbers, magnificent artichokes, colourful-stalked Swiss chard, beans in various shapes and colours –not to mention the full glory of summer vegetable delights.

It continues in autumn with pumpkin and potatoes, parsnips and parsley root, before I then enjoy the hearty vegetables of winter: leeks, swede, salsify, and Jerusalem artichokes. And of course cabbage – Brussels sprouts, kale, black cabbage, savoy, white, and red cabbage. There's no chance of vegetable boredom here!

SEASONAL, ORGANIC, REGIONAL

Do I even need to mention that – besides seasonality – it's very important to me that vegetables and co. come from organic farming or, otherwise, from regional sources? If you've read this far, you've probably already guessed it, haven't you?

GRAINS –
NOT A DAY WITHOUT GRAINS

Are we even aware of how often we eat grains? It starts with breakfast: bread or rolls, muesli or warm porridge. It continues at lunch: pizza or pasta, paella or pancakes, dumplings or sushi, bulgur salad or Korean bibimbap – grains are in all of them, whether as flour, semolina, or whole kernels. Even the slice of cake, the waffles, or the cookies in the afternoon don't go without flour. And what would a proper dinner be without – exactly – bread, or rolls?

SOURCE OF ENERGY

Grains are one of our most important sources of nutrients. Grains consist of 60–70 per cent carbohydrates. They also contain 10–15 per cent protein.

In addition, grains provide dietary fibre, minerals, and vitamins – primarily B vitamins. The fibre helps, among other things, to ensure that the blood sugar level rises only slowly. Fibre is especially found in whole grains – so feel free to reach more often for whole grains or whole grain flour. The latter is available from many types of grain: wheat, einkorn, emmer, spelt, or rye.

ANCIENT GRAINS

Grains have been cultivated for many thousands of years. Einkorn, emmer, kamut (Khorasan wheat), spelt, and barley are even referred to as ancient grains. It's wonderful that these old grain varieties have been increasingly cultivated again in organic agriculture in recent years. From a nutritional standpoint, ancient grains can outperform wheat with a higher content of certain minerals and proteins. They also contribute to a greater diversity of flavours. And even though these ancient grain varieties have been selectively bred especially in terms of yield and quality, they remain niche products in the wheat-dominated grain market. That also explains their significantly higher price.

SEMOLINA, GRITS, BARLEY & CO.

Grain is mostly ground into flour, but it is also processed into semolina, grits, barley, flakes, cracked grain, and bran.

Semolina is mostly made from wheat, but also from spelt, corn (polenta), and millet.

Grits are sized between semolina and barley. For this, the grain kernels are steamed and then crushed using a drum grits cutter. The most well-known is buckwheat grits.

For barley, the husks of barley kernels are removed, the kernels are peeled and polished. Barley is also sold under the names 'rolled barley' or 'cooking barley.'

As fine or coarse flakes, oats most often end up in our muesli, but flakes are also made from spelt, rye, buckwheat, barley, or einkorn.

DRINKS AND OIL

Grains are used to make caffeine-free grain coffee, and even other drinks rely on grains – think of brewing malt from barley for beer production, or high-proof spirits like Korn (grain schnapps) and the like. Oil is also pressed from the wheat germ, which is removed when grinding the wheat kernels, and sold as wheat germ oil.

EMMER
GREEN SPELT
FREEKEH
COUSCOUS
CRACKED GREEN SPELT
EINKORN FLOUR
EINKORN

SPELT SEMOLINA
PEARL COUSCOUS
SPELT FLAKES
SPELT
WHEAT
KAMUT FLOUR
SEMOLINA
KAMUT
BULGUR

WHEAT

WITHOUT WHEAT, THERE IS NOTHING

Wheat is on everyone's lips, and that's true worldwide. That's reason enough to give this grain a prominent place here.

Wheat is one of the oldest cultivated plants in the world. It was grown in the Near East as early as 8,000–10,000 years ago. What we now refer to as ancient wheat – such as emmer, einkorn, and kamut/Khorasan wheat – was first cultivated in Europe in the Mediterranean region. Alongside rice and corn, wheat is one of the most important foods in global nutrition.

Wheat is grown on all continents. Its cultivation is increasing globally, with a large portion of the harvest – like corn – not used directly for human consumption but as animal feed. In addition to ancient wheat varieties, the wheat family also includes spelt and green spelt.

OUR DAILY BREAD

Wheat plays a particularly important role as bread grain. In many countries, bread is one of the most essential staple foods and is baked all over the world. Bread is primarily made from various types of wheat, each with specific requirements for climate and soil. Cold-resistant winter wheat is by far the most widely cultivated and is sown in the autumn. In colder regions, the more delicate spring wheat is often sown in the spring. Both types are harvested in the summer.

HARD AND SOFT WHEAT

Hard and soft wheat are different wheat varieties that differ not only in appearance but also in their uses. Soft wheat is the most commonly grown wheat worldwide. It is primarily milled into flour to bake bread, rolls, and sweet pastries – hence its nickname 'bread wheat'.

Hard wheat, also known as durum wheat, is slightly yellowish and has a higher gluten (glue protein) content, making it particularly suitable for pasta production. Both in processing and cooking, pasta made from durum holds its shape well and remains firm to the bite – just the way we like it.

Depending on the degree of milling, various foods can be made from durum wheat, ranging from very fine durum flour for pasta to semolina, and coarser grains like couscous and bulgur.

SPELT, GREEN SPELT, AND FREEKEH

Spelt is closely related to modern wheat. Due to its lower yield, it was almost entirely displaced by the more productive wheat, but in recent years, it has been cultivated more widely again. Spelt is better suited to rougher climates than wheat. It is more labour-intensive and expensive to process because the spelt grains are tightly enclosed in a woody husk (the hull), making them difficult to separate. There are many hybrid forms between spelt and wheat. To what extent these modern hybrids match the quality of traditional spelt remains unclear.

Green spelt is spelt that is harvested unripe and kiln-dried. This practice originated from necessity – spelt grains were harvested before full ripeness during bad weather – but it continued because the green, dried grains taste so good. Green spelt is available as whole grain and often as groats.

Freekeh is especially known in Levantine cuisine and is still relatively uncommon in our region. Freekeh is unripe durum wheat that is dried and roasted over fire, giving it a delicate, smoky flavour.

AND WHAT ABOUT GLUTEN?

Few foods have come under fire in recent years as much as wheat. Wheat- and gluten-free foods are growing in popularity. Those who must follow a gluten-free diet due to illnesses like coeliac disease or other chronic conditions need to avoid all gluten-containing foods strictly to alleviate symptoms.

GLUTEN-FREE GRAINS

People with gluten sensitivity also benefit from a gluten-free diet, even if it's often not gluten itself but other proteins that cause discomfort.

Fortunately, there is a wide variety of gluten-free grains like buckwheat, amaranth, quinoa, corn, rice, and millet. Good news: some gluten-free pseudo-grains like quinoa and amaranth, which originate from South America, are increasingly being cultivated elsewhere as well. Growing demand – and unfortunately also climate change – makes it possible for these healthy grains to reach our markets without long transport routes.

RISOTTO RICE (CARNAROLI)
PAELLA
SHORT GRAIN RICE
WILD RICE
MIXED WILD RICE
BLACK RICE
PUDDING RICE

BROWN RICE
RED CAMARGUE RICE
BASMATI RICE
JASMIN RICE
SUSHI RICE

RICE

RICE – BROWN, WHITE, BLACK, OR RED

Especially in Asia – notably in China, India, and Southeast Asia – rice is a daily staple on plates or in bowls. For more than half of the world's population, rice is the primary food source.

Rice cultivation in Asia has a tradition going back thousands of years; over 90 percent of the global harvest is still grown there today. In contrast, rice cultivation plays only a very small role in Europe. The main growing areas here are northern Italy (the Po Valley), as well as Portugal, Spain, and France (Camargue). Rice is also cultivated – though to a much smaller extent – in Greece, Switzerland, and Austria. Unlike Asian rice, rice grown in Europe is marketed and consumed only within Europe, meaning that the transport routes are relatively short in comparison.

ORYZA SATIVA

The rice plant *Oryza sativa* belongs to the grass family (*Poaceae*). These are annual plants that must be replanted each year. When we think of rice cultivation, we usually picture terraced rice fields. The so-called wet cultivation – that is, the flooding of rice fields – has a long tradition and accounts for around 80 percent of rice production.

Flooding the fields prevents weeds and pests from growing, as the rice plants tolerate being flooded without damage. After irrigation, the rice fields are drained, and the rice plants are harvested – predominantly by hand. Depending on the variety and growing region, one to three harvests per year are possible. This conventional rice farming method is increasingly criticized for its ecological impact – due to high water consumption and the release of methane. In addition to the widespread wet cultivation, rice is also grown dry, just like other grains. However, dry cultivation is much more labour-intensive and yields less; farmers must deal with more weeds and pests than in flooded fields, so dry-grown rice is not seen as a viable solution on a global scale.

RICE HARVEST

To obtain the rice grains, the mature panicles are threshed. They are still enclosed in the straw-like husk, the hull, and are not edible in this form. In this state, rice is referred to as raw rice or paddy rice. The husks are then removed, leaving the actual rice grain, which consists of the starchy endosperm, the germ, and the silver skin. This rice is called cargo rice and can be exported. It enters the market as brown rice, whole grain rice, or natural rice.

FROM BROWN TO WHITE RICE

A large part of the rice harvest is subsequently milled and polished, which removes the germ and silver skin. The resulting white rice has a longer shelf life than the unmilled, brown rice, because the fatty germ has been removed. A major disadvantage of milling is that it causes the loss of minerals and vitamins.

In the parboiling process, the unmilled cargo rice is soaked and then treated with hot steam under pressure. This causes many important nutrients to be pushed into the interior of the grain, where they remain even after milling and polishing.

All rice varieties are gluten-free and especially rich in B vitamins. Unmilled brown rice contains significantly more vitamins and minerals than white, i.e. milled and polished, rice.

LONG AND SHORT, ROUND AND SLENDER

Rice is usually categorised based on the size and shape of the grain: long grain, medium grain, and short grain.

LONG GRAIN RICE

In long grain rice, the grains stay separate when cooked; they don't stick together or only minimally. Some of the most popular long grain varieties include the aromatic, fragrant basmati rice, which comes from the Himalayan region.

Jasmine rice, from Thailand, releases its delicate fragrance during cooking. Vietnamese sticky rice is mainly used for desserts, such as sticky rice. Parboiled rice and brown rice also belong to the large group of long grain rice varieties. For quick-cooking rice, the rice is pre-cooked and then dried again, although this process causes it to lose some of its flavour.

SHORT GRAIN RICE

Short grain rice grains become sticky when cooked because they release a lot of starch. These varieties are suitable for sushi or rice pudding, risotto or paella. What we buy as sushi rice is a Japanese short grain rice that holds its shape well after cooking.

Risotto rice is a general term for several short grain rice varieties, the most well-known being Arborio, Vialone, and Carnaroli. These grains are round to medium in length and absorb a lot of liquid during cooking, resulting in a creamy risotto.

Spanish bomba rice – *arroz bomba* – is traditionally used for Valencian paella. It contains less starch than other short grain varieties, so it remains firmer and grainier when cooked.

WILD RICE

The brown, long grains are botanically not rice, but the seeds of a grass species that grows near lakes and rivers in the USA and Canada. These rather expensive, nutritious grains have a delicate, nutty flavour and should be gently cooked to prevent them from bursting too much.

UNIQUE RICE VARIETIES

Among the more unusual varieties are red rice, a natural rice with a red bran layer. It's grown in the Camargue region of southern France, but also in Asia.

Green rice is grown mainly in Vietnam and harvested before full maturity, which preserves its green colour. You can find green rice in Asian grocery stores – it's mainly used for breading.

Black rice originates from China and is now grown mainly in Asia. *Riso venere* (Venus rice) is a cross between black rice and an Italian variety and is now cultivated in Piedmont and also in France. The grains of this whole grain rice variety are white on the inside and remain very firm even after long cooking. They have a strong, distinctive flavour.

BREAKFAST

QUINOA GRANOLA WITH RHUBARB COMPOTE

Once you've started making your own granola, you'll be reluctant to go back to store-bought muesli, which is usually heavily sweetened. You can swap the multigrain flakes as you wish – try oat, einkorn, or spelt flakes.

SERVES 8
VEGAN

QUINOA GRANOLA
25 g hazelnuts
125 g multigrain flakes
30 g puffed quinoa
1 tbsp sesame seeds
2 tsp cocoa powder
½ tsp ground cinnamon
50 g tahini (sesame paste)
60 g maple syrup
40 ml vegetable oil

RHUBARB COMPOTE
500 g rhubarb
approx. 50 g sugar
200 g raspberries (fresh or frozen)

ALSO
400 g plant yogurt (e.g. coconut yogurt)

Preheat the oven to 180°C/160°C fan. Line a baking tray with parchment paper.

Roughly chop the hazelnuts. Mix with multigrain flakes, quinoa, sesame seeds, cocoa, and cinnamon in a bowl. In a small saucepan, gently warm the tahini with the maple syrup and oil, and stir well. Add to the flake mixture and mix thoroughly. Spread evenly on the baking tray and bake in the middle of the preheated oven for about 20 minutes, stirring once after 10 minutes. Remove at the end of baking time and let cool completely.

For the rhubarb compote, clean the rhubarb and cut into short pieces. Place in a pot with 100 ml water and the sugar, and bring to a boil. Cook for about 2 minutes, then add the raspberries and cook the compote for another 1–2 minutes.

Divide the (warm or cooled) compote among bowls, add yogurt and some quinoa granola. Store the rest of the granola in an airtight jar – it keeps for at least 2 weeks.

PREPARATION TIME: 30 minutes plus 20 minutes baking

OVERNIGHT OATS WITH CHIA AND BERRIES

How convenient: simply prepare everything the evening before, fill into jars, and the next day you can look forward to a delicious breakfast – that's how to start the day right. If it's not berry season, then I serve the oats with other seasonal fruits.

SERVES 4

VEGAN

OVERNIGHT OATS

150 g coarse rolled oats

4 tbsp chia seeds (20 g)

300 ml plant milk (e.g. oat milk)

300 g plant yogurt (e.g. oat yogurt)

FOR SERVING

4 tbsp plant yogurt (e.g. oat yogurt)

250 g mixed berries

2–3 tbsp white almond butter

4 tbsp maple syrup

2 tsp chia seeds for sprinkling

For the overnight oats, stir together oats, chia seeds, plant milk, and plant yogurt and place covered in the refrigerator overnight.

The next morning, stir again, divide into four bowls, and top with yogurt. Carefully wash the berries, let them drain, and place them on top. Finish with almond butter, maple syrup, and chia seeds.

PREPARATION TIME: 10 minutes plus 30 minutes for soaking and 1 night for resting

CHOCOLATE BUCKWHEAT PORRIDGE WITH PLUMS

Especially when it's cold in the morning, I love starting the day with a warm porridge. In winter, I replace the fresh plums with stewed ones, apple sauce, or quince compote.

SERVES 4

VEGAN

PORRIDGE

300 g buckwheat

approx. 700 ml plant milk (e.g. oat milk)

1 pinch of salt

2 tbsp cocoa powder

3 tbsp maple syrup

2 tsp gingerbread spice or ground cinnamon

TOPPING

2 tbsp buckwheat

8 plums

2 tbsp blackcurrant jelly

250 g plant yogurt (e.g. coconut yogurt)

Rinse the buckwheat in a sieve under cold running water and drain. In a pot, combine buckwheat, plant milk, salt, cocoa powder, maple syrup, and gingerbread spice or cinnamon. Bring to a boil. Simmer over low heat for 8 minutes, stirring occasionally, then let it swell for another 5-10 minutes.

Meanwhile, toast the buckwheat for the topping in a pan for 3-5 minutes until golden brown, then set aside. Halve and pit the plums, then simmer in a small pot with the blackcurrant jelly and 5 tbsp water for 2-3 minutes until soft.

Stir the porridge and, if necessary, add some oat milk or water until the porridge has a thick, creamy consistency. Divide into bowls, top with yogurt and plums, and sprinkle with toasted buckwheat.

PREPARATION TIME: 30 minutes

AMARANTH PORRIDGE WITH HAZELNUTS AND APPLES

Amaranth belongs to the group of pseudo-grains. The small, gluten-free grains are very rich in protein and packed with minerals and healthy secondary plant compounds. One more reason to start the day with this delicious porridge!

SERVES 4

VEGAN

PORRIDGE

300 g amaranth
4 tbsp ground hazelnuts
600–700 ml plant milk (e.g. oat milk)
1 pinch of salt

TOPPING

4 tbsp hazelnut flakes
2 tart apples
1–2 tbsp butter or non-dairy alternative
4 tbsp liquid honey or agave nectar
2 tbsp puffed amaranth (amaranth pops)

Rinse the amaranth in a fine sieve under cold running water and let it drain.

Briefly roast the ground hazelnuts in a pot until they are lightly browned. Deglaze with plant milk. Add the amaranth and salt, bring to a boil, and simmer gently over low heat for 20-25 minutes, stirring occasionally. Remove the pot from the heat and let the porridge swell for a few more minutes.

For the topping, toast the hazelnut flakes in a pan without fat until golden brown and set aside.

Core the apples using an apple corer and cut crosswise into thin slices. Heat the butter in a wide pan and sauté the apples for about 2 minutes over medium heat. Drizzle with honey and briefly caramelise. Remove from the heat.

Stir the porridge briefly. If it's too thick, stir in a bit more plant milk. Spoon the porridge into bowls, top with apples, and sprinkle with toasted hazelnut flakes and puffed amaranth.

PREPARATION TIME: 15 minutes plus 20–25 minutes cooking

ONE BOWL

SALADS TO FILL YOU UP

FRESH AND CRUNCHY, ABUNDANT AND SATISFYING

SPELT SALAD WITH TOMATOES, FENNEL, AND PESTO DRESSING

Spelt is one of those grains that you should soak for several hours beforehand to shorten the long cooking time. You can also cook it in a pressure cooker – that saves time and energy. Let the salad rest sufficiently before eating, so the spelt grains can absorb the flavours of the dressing.

SERVES 4
VEGAN

150 g spelt grains
Salt
1 small fennel bulb
4 large tomatoes

DRESSING
1 tsp fennel seeds
4 tbsp lemon juice
2–3 tbsp vegan basil pesto
Salt
Black pepper from the mill
5 tbsp olive oil

ALSO
1 small head of radicchio

Soak the spelt in a pot with plenty of water the day before. The next day, drain the water, bring the spelt to a boil in fresh salted water, and cook for about 20 minutes. Drain in a sieve, rinse under cold water, and let it drain.

Clean the fennel and slice it thinly; finely chop the fennel greens. Cut the tomatoes into thin wedges.

For the dressing: Crush the fennel seeds in a mortar, then mix with lemon juice, pesto, a bit of salt, pepper, and olive oil. Combine spelt, fennel, fennel greens, tomatoes, and dressing. Let it sit, covered, for at least 2 hours.

Shortly before serving, clean and wash the radicchio, spin dry, tear into pieces, and mix into the salad. Taste and adjust seasoning if necessary.

PREPARATION TIME: 25 minutes plus overnight soaking and 2 hours resting

TIP It's faster with parboiled spelt. You can buy it as 'spelt-like rice' or 'spelt rice' – it doesn't need to be soaked.

COLOURFUL SUSHI BOWL

Especially in summer, I love a chirashi bowl – that's what sushi bowls are called in Japan. The toppings are almost endlessly variable. I usually just see what's ready to harvest in the garden – your imagination is the only limit.

SERVES 4

VEGAN

RICE

400 g sushi rice
3 tbsp light vinegar (rice or white wine vinegar)
2 tsp sugar
Salt

TOPPING

150 g edamame beans
Salt
1 candy-striped beetroot
1 ripe avocado
2 radishes
1 sheet nori

SAUCE

4 tbsp vegan mayonnaise
Approx. 2 tbsp lime juice
2 tsp agave syrup
3–5 tsp wasabi paste

ALSO

2 tbsp cress
4 tsp pickled sushi ginger
1 tbsp each light and black sesame seeds

Put the sushi rice in a sieve and rinse under cold running water until the water runs clear, then drain. Bring to a boil with 800 ml water and cook for 10 minutes. Then let it swell over low heat for 20 minutes. Meanwhile, mix the vinegar with 2 tablespoons of cold water, sugar, and just over ½ teaspoon of salt. Stir into the cooked rice, then transfer to a bowl and let cool.

For the topping: Cook the edamame beans in salted water for 2–3 minutes until tender, then drain, rinse under cold water, and drain again. Peel the candy-striped beetrootand slice thinly. Halve and pit the avocado, peel it, and cut the flesh into slices. Halve the radishes. Cut the nori sheet into thin strips with scissors.

For the sauce: Mix the mayonnaise, lime juice, agave syrup, and wasabi paste. Stir in water by the spoonful until the sauce has a thick consistency.

Divide the rice between four bowls, arrange the toppings, cress, pickled ginger, and sauce on top, and sprinkle with sesame seeds.

PREPARATION TIME: 45 minutes

BULGUR SALAD WITH FETA AND POMEGRANATE

A trip to the Turkish or Arab grocery store, and you've got all the ingredients for this salad, which comes from Turkey: fine bulgur, aromatic pepper paste, Pul Biber (mild or hot chilli flakes), tangy pomegranate syrup, and feta, of course alongside fresh vegetables and fragrant herbs!

SERVES 4
VEGAN

200 g fine bulgur
Salt
250 g cherry tomatoes
½ cucumber
1 red onion
1 bunch flat leaf parsley
1 bunch mint
½ pomegranate

DRESSING
2 untreated lemons
2 tbsp pomegranate syrup
1 heaped tbsp hot pepper paste
5 tbsp olive oil
1 tsp Pul Biber (chilli flakes)
Salt

200 g feta or vegan feta, for topping

Cook the bulgur in 500 ml of boiling salted water for 2 minutes, then remove the pot from the heat and let the bulgur swell and cool down.

Meanwhile, halve the tomatoes and finely dice the cucumber. Peel the onion, halve it, and cut into thin strips. Rinse the herbs, shake dry, and finely chop both the soft stems and the leaves. Remove the seeds from the pomegranate.

For the dressing: Wash the lemons in hot water, dry, finely grate the peel, and squeeze the juice. Mix lemon juice and zest with pomegranate syrup, pepper paste, olive oil, pul biber, and a bit of salt.

Mix all prepared ingredients together and let the salad rest for 1–2 hours in a cool place.

Before serving, crumble the feta and gently fold it in. Taste the bulgur salad again and adjust seasoning if necessary.

PREPARATION TIME: 35 minutes plus 1–2 hours resting

TRADITIONAL CRAFTSMANSHIP, MODERN TECHNOLOGY

The old folk song line comes to mind as we stand in front of the Bohlsen mill, a beautiful old brick building: '*The mill clatters by the rushing stream...*'

Because the Bohlsen mill, located in the middle of the Lüneburg Heath, is not just named like a mill – it truly is one, and in fact, a water mill. It stands right in the village, in a place where grain has been ground for centuries; a mill already stood here in the 13th century. It remains the economic centre of this Lower Saxony village. Right next to the imposing brick structure flows the Gerdau, a small river. Every second, two cubic metres of water transfer their power to turbines that drive the roller mills on the upper floor of the building.

Although the river's fluctuating water level no longer reliably supplies enough energy on its own, the sight alone transports us to another time – another century. This feeling only deepens upon entering the mill: there's rattling and rumbling, banging and whistling. The mill is alive, working hard, the wide wooden floorboards vibrating under our feet. And the scent of freshly ground grain fills the air.

Bohlsen mill processes all types of grains and pseudo-cereals into flour and semolina, flakes and groats. In addition to classic grains like wheat and oats, they also mill ancient varieties like einkorn, emmer, and spelt, as well as pseudo-cereals such as amaranth, buckwheat, and quinoa – twenty-two types in total.

Around two hundred organic-certified (Bioland) farmers from the region deliver their grain several times a week – true to the mill owners' motto since the late 1970s: 'Every hectare farmed organically is a gain for people and nature.'

Before grains like spelt, emmer, or millet become flour, they pass through fourteen milling stations. The grains are broken down into fine, medium, and coarse parts – into light and dark components – and rush through a tangle of pipes on the pipe floor of the mill's second story.

Flour, semolina, groats, flakes, and bran all pass through this 'pipe forest', and through small viewing windows, you can peek inside the pipes, marvelling – and only beginning to grasp – just how complex the work of a modern-day miller really is.

And even though the technology inside the old mill has completely changed – old roller mills have been replaced by modern systems (the oldest roller mill dates back to the 1930s and still performs its job reliably) – you can still sense the spirit of the old mill. For many years, it has done its work, weathered difficult times, constantly adapted – and it still lives on today, right in the heart of the small village.

RICE SALAD WITH MANGO AND CASHEWS

When I cook rice, wheat, and co., I usually make a double portion and enjoy the generous 'leftovers' the next or the following day in a new dish. That not only saves time but also valuable energy!

SERVES 4
VEGAN

200 g jasmine rice
Salt
100 g sugar snap peas
200 g carrots
½ bunch spring onions
⅓ cucumber
1 red onion
1 ripe mango
1 large bunch coriander
½ bunch mint

DRESSING
20 g fresh ginger
1 clove garlic
4–5 tbsp lime juice
2 tbsp brown sugar
2–3 tsp sambal oelek
4 tbsp vegetable oil
4–5 tbsp light soy sauce

ALSO
50 g roasted, salted cashew nuts

Cook the rice according to packet instructions in salted water until al dente. Drain in a sieve, rinse with cold water, and let it drain.

Blanch the sugar snap peas briefly in boiling salted water, drain, rinse cold, and let them drain as well.

Brush the carrots under running water and cut them into fine strips or coarsely grate them. Clean the spring onions and cut into fine rings. Halve the cucumber lengthwise, remove the seeds, and cut into thin slices. Peel the red onion and cut into thin wedges. Peel the mango, remove the flesh from the pit, and dice. Rinse the herbs, shake them dry, and coarsely chop both soft stems and leaves.

For the dressing: Peel and finely chop the ginger and garlic. Mix the lime juice and brown sugar until the sugar dissolves. Stir in ginger, garlic, sambal oelek, oil, a bit of salt, and soy sauce.

Mix rice, vegetables, mango, and herbs with the dressing and let sit for 15 minutes.

Roughly chop the cashews. Taste the salad and sprinkle with the cashews before serving.

PREPARATION TIME: 45 minutes plus 15 minutes resting

GREEN ASPARAGUS WITH BUCKWHEAT CRUNCH, GOAT CHEESE, AND STRAWBERRY VINAIGRETTE

It's wonderful that asparagus and strawberries share the spring season – they go together beautifully on the plate and on the palate! I usually roast a double batch of the buckwheat crunch, since I also like to sprinkle it over leafy salads.

SERVES 4
VEGAN

BUCKWHEAT CRUNCH
50 g hazelnuts
50 g whole buckwheat
50 g rolled oats
3 tbsp olive oil
1 tbsp honey or agave syrup
2 tsp whole grain mustard
Salt
Black pepper from the mill

SALAD
250 g strawberries
3-4 tbsp lemon juice
2 tsp honey or agave syrup
4 tbsp olive oil
Salt
Black pepper from the mill
500 g green asparagus
150-200 g goat cheese log or plant-based alternative

ALSO
1 handful of herbs (e.g. nasturtium, marjoram blossoms)

For the buckwheat crunch: Preheat the oven to 180°C/160°C fan. Line a baking sheet with parchment paper. Coarsely chop the hazelnuts and mix with buckwheat, rolled oats, olive oil, honey, mustard, salt, and pepper. Spread the mixture onto the baking sheet and bake in the preheated oven for 15–20 minutes until crispy and golden brown. Remove and let cool – the crunch will firm up as it cools.

Clean the strawberries. For the vinaigrette: Purée 2-3 strawberries with lemon juice, honey, and olive oil. Season with salt and pepper.

Slice the remaining strawberries. Trim the ends of the asparagus and peel the lower third. In a wide pot, bring about 3 cm of salted water to a boil. Add the asparagus and steam for 2-3 minutes until tender-crisp. Lift out, rinse with cold water, and drain well. Save the asparagus water for a soup or risotto.

Slice the goat cheese. Arrange the asparagus and cheese on plates. Drizzle with the vinaigrette, then top with the buckwheat crunch and herbs.

PREPARATION TIME: 25 minutes plus 15–20 minutes baking

PINK COUSCOUS SALAD WITH RADISHES AND DILL

Once the beetroot is cooked, this simple, colourful salad is ready in no time and already lifts your mood just by looking at it – and with every bite, it gets even better. Promise!

SERVES 4

500 g beetroot (preferably small)
Salt
250 g couscous
½ bunch radishes
½ bunch dill
1 untreated lemon
2 tbsp balsamic vinegar
Freshly ground black pepper
2 tsp liquid honey or agave syrup
Approx. 5 tbsp olive oil
200 g Greek yogurt or plant-based alternative

Scrub the beetroot well under running water and cook them unpeeled in lightly salted water for 45–60 minutes until tender.

Meanwhile, mix the couscous with 250 ml cold water and a bit of salt, let it soak for a few minutes.

Trim and wash the radishes, reserve some attractive leaves, and slice the radishes thinly.

Pluck the dill fronds and finely chop them. Wash the lemon in hot water, pat dry, finely grate the zest, and squeeze the juice.

In a bowl, vigorously whisk together 4–5 tablespoons lemon juice, lemon zest, 2 tablespoons balsamic vinegar, a bit of salt, plenty of black pepper, 2 teaspoons honey, and about 5 tablespoons olive oil.

Once the beetroot are cooked (check with a small knife), drain them, rinse with cold water, peel, and slice into thin wedges.

While still warm, mix the beetroot wedges with the couscous and the dressing – the couscous gradually takes on a pink colour. Let the salad cool, then stir in the radish slices and leaves, and the dill.

Before serving, taste again and adjust seasoning – does it need more acidity or spice? Serve with smooth Greek yogurt spooned on top.

PREPARATION TIME: 35 minutes, cooking time: 45–60 minutes

PEARL COUSCOUS SALAD WITH SPINACH, PRESERVED LEMON, AND HALLOUMI

Pearl couscous is also known as Israeli couscous or Ptitim. Unlike the finely granulated couscous, it's not a grain, but a toasted wheat product that looks like small pasta pearls. It has a pleasantly nutty flavour and a firm bite – and tastes especially good in this summery salad with apricots, mint, and salty halloumi.

SERVES 4
VEGAN

SALAD
250 g pearl couscous
Salt
½ cucumber
½ bunch spring onions
1 bunch mint
1 small red chilli
75 g dried apricots
½ preserved lemon
Approx. 2 tsp Ras el-Hanout
50 g baby spinach
2 tbsp almonds
250 g halloumi or plant-based alternative
1 tbsp olive oil for frying

DRESSING
4 tbsp lemon juice
4 tbsp olive oil
1–2 tsp honey or agave syrup
Salt
Freshly ground pepper

Cook the couscous in boiling salted water according to the packet instructions. Drain in a sieve, rinse with cold water, and let it drain well.

Meanwhile, halve the cucumber lengthwise, remove the seeds, and slice the halves into thin slices. Clean the spring onions and cut them into fine rings. Rinse the mint, pat it dry, and coarsely chop the thin stems and leaves. Deseed and finely chop the chilli. Coarsely chop the apricots. Quarter the preserved lemon, remove the flesh from the peel, and cut only the peel into very thin strips.

Loosen up the couscous and place it in a bowl with the cucumber, spring onions, mint, chilli, apricots, preserved lemon, and Ras el-Hanout.

For the dressing: Vigorously whisk together lemon juice, 2 tablespoons of the preserved lemon brine, olive oil, honey, a little salt, and pepper, then stir it into the salad. Cover and let the salad marinate for at least 2 hours.

Wash and spin dry the spinach. Coarsely chop the almonds and lightly toast them in a dry pan, then remove and let cool. Pat the halloumi dry and slice it into pieces just under 1 cm thick. Heat the olive oil in a pan and briefly sear the halloumi on both sides until golden brown.

Mix the spinach and almonds into the salad, season to taste, and adjust if necessary. Serve with the halloumi on top.

PREPARATION TIME: 40 minutes plus 2 hours marinating time

CHICORY WITH ASIAN WILD RICE FILLING

Wild rice, with its long, dark grains, comes from water-rich areas of North America and Canada and is a type of grass. The nutty-tasting, healthy grains are rich in protein and minerals, which I love to combine with Asian flavours.

SERVES 4
VEGAN

150 g wild rice
Salt
1 red onion
1 clove garlic
15 g fresh ginger
200 g carrots
1 small kohlrabi
150 g brown mushrooms
½ bunch coriander
75 g roasted, salted peanuts
2 tbsp toasted sesame oil
2 tbsp vegetable oil
3-4 tbsp light soy sauce
2 tsp chilli flakes
2 heads chicory

Cook the wild rice in salted water over low heat for about 45 minutes, then drain in a sieve and let drip off.

Meanwhile, peel the onion, garlic, and ginger. Cut the onion into thin strips, finely chop the garlic and ginger. Peel the carrots and kohlrabi and grate or shave them into thin strips. Clean the mushrooms and slice them thinly. Rinse the coriander, shake it dry, chop thin stems and leaves finely. Roughly chop the peanuts.

Heat sesame oil and vegetable oil in a wok or wide pan and sauté onion, kohlrabi, carrots, and mushrooms over medium heat for about 5 minutes. Add garlic and ginger and briefly sauté. Deglaze with soy sauce. Mix in wild rice, coriander, and half the peanuts, and season with a little salt and 1 teaspoon chilli flakes.

Separate the chicory into individual leaves, wash and pat dry, then place in a bowl. Spoon the vegetable mixture onto the chicory leaves and sprinkle with the remaining peanuts and the rest of the chilli flakes.

PREPARATION TIME: 30 minutes plus 45 minutes cooking

MARINATED CARROTS WITH OATS, LABNEH AND APRICOT SAUCE

You don't need to soak oat grains, they cook relatively quickly. The labneh, a creamy fresh cheese, takes a bit more time – one or even better two days to drain. Only then does it become nicely thick and creamy. Greek cream yogurt is a quick vegetarian alternative.

SERVES 4

VEGAN

LABNEH

600 g plant-based yogurt (preferably oat or soy)
1 tbsp lemon juice
1 tsp finely grated zest from an untreated lemon
1 tsp maple syrup
1 tbsp olive oil
½ tsp salt

SALAD

150 g oat grains
Salt
50 g hazelnuts
3 bay leaves
1 bunch carrots (approx. 500 g)

SAUCE

2 tbsp apricot fruit spread
4 tbsp lemon juice
1 tsp chilli flakes
5 tbsp olive oil

ALSO

1 handful herb and salad leaves (e.g. basil, mustard, Asian salad)

One to two days beforehand, line a sieve with a (paper) kitchen towel and place it over a bowl. Stir together the yogurt, lemon juice, lemon zest, maple syrup, olive oil, and salt. Pour into the sieve, cover, and let drain in the fridge.

Place the oat grains in a pot, cover with water, add salt, bring to a boil and cook for 20–30 minutes. Then pour the oats into a sieve and let drain. Toast the hazelnuts briefly in a dry pan, place in a kitchen towel and rub off as much skin as possible, then roughly chop.

In a wide pot, bring salted water with bay leaves to a boil. Trim the carrot tops and peel the carrots. Cook the carrots in boiling water for 5–7 minutes until al dente, then remove.

For the sauce: Whisk together apricot fruit spread, lemon juice, chilli flakes, a little salt and the olive oil. Drizzle the warm carrots with the sauce and let marinate for at least 30 minutes.

To serve, spread the labneh on a plate, arrange the marinated carrots with the sauce and oats on top. Sprinkle with chopped hazelnuts and herb and salad leaves.

PREPARATION TIME: 30 minutes plus 2 days draining, 20-30 minutes cooking, and 30 minutes marinating

SALAD BOWL WITH SUMMER ROLLS AND PEANUT SAUCE

I find preparing summer rolls wonderfully relaxing. Use whatever vegetables your garden or fridge has to offer. That way, they taste a little different every time – but always good!

SERVES 4

VEGAN

SALAD AND ROLLS

100 g multicolour quinoa

Salt

2–3 handfuls of leafy salad

1 small carrot

1 small kohlrabi or yellow beetroot

1 mini cucumber

2 spring onions

1 large handful each of coriander and mint

2 tbsp roasted, salted peanuts

approx. 20 rice paper sheets

SAUCE

1 clove garlic

1 small piece ginger (approx. 20 g)

½ small red chilli

2 tbsp roasted, salted peanuts

125 g peanut butter

3 tbsp light soy sauce

3 tbsp lime juice

1 tbsp brown sugar

Rinse quinoa thoroughly under cold water in a sieve, then cook in salted water for about 10 minutes. Drain, let cool.

Meanwhile, for the sauce, peel and chop garlic and ginger. Seed and chop the chilli. Blend garlic, ginger, chilli, peanuts, 3–5 tbsp water, and remaining ingredients with an immersion blender. Set aside.

For the salad and filling: Wash and pat dry the salad leaves. Scrub or peel the carrot under cold running water, peel the kohlrabi or beetroot. Cut vegetables into fine, uniform sticks. Clean the spring onions and cut into thin rings. Wash and dry the herbs, finely chop stems and leaves. Roughly chop the peanuts.

Soak one rice paper sheet at a time in a wide bowl or large frying pan of cold water for about 1 minute, remove, shake off water, and lay on work surface.

Place 1–2 salad leaves in the centre of each sheet, then about 1 tbsp quinoa, prepared vegetables, herbs, and peanuts. Drizzle with 1 tsp sauce. Fold in the sides of the rice paper over the filling and roll up tightly. Repeat for all rolls.

Distribute the remaining salad into bowls. Halve the summer rolls crosswise and place them in the bowls with the remaining sauce.

PREPARATION TIME: 50 minutes plus 10 minutes cooking

SNACKS

SMALL CHEESE SCONES

These hearty, flaky scones are great for an apéro and are best eaten on the same day.

MAKES ABOUT 24 PIECES

1 egg (size M)
110 g yogurt (3.5% fat)
60 g strong cheese
225 g spelt flour (Type 630) plus extra for rolling
2 tbsp fine spelt flakes
1 tsp baking powder
1 tsp sugar
½ tsp salt
60 g cold butter
1 egg yolk (size M)
2 tbsp fine spelt flakes for sprinkling

Preheat the oven to 200°C/180°C fan. Line a baking tray with parchment paper.

Whisk the egg and yogurt, finely grate the cheese and add. Mix spelt flour, spelt flakes, baking powder, sugar, and salt in a mixing bowl. Add the butter in small cubes and the egg mixture, and work in with your fingers until coarse crumbs form. Roll out the dough about 2 cm thick on a lightly floured surface.

Cut out small circles about 4 cm in diameter and place them on the prepared tray. Briefly knead the dough scraps together, roll out again, and cut out more circles. Mix the egg yolk and 2 teaspoons of water, brush the dough circles with it, and sprinkle with spelt flakes. Bake in the preheated oven for 12–15 minutes until golden brown. Remove and let cool.

PREPARATION TIME: 30 minutes plus 12–15 minutes baking

TENDER PESTO CRESCENTS

There's no skimping on butter and cream cheese here – only this makes the crescents nicely tender. They taste best fresh but also keep well for a few days in a tin.

MAKES ABOUT 24 PIECES

- 100 g soft butter
- 100 g cream cheese (full-fat)
- 75 g wheat flour (Type 405) plus flour for rolling
- 75 g wholewheat flour
- ½ tsp salt
- 3 tbsp basil or other herb pesto
- 4 tbsp grated Parmesan (40 g)
- 1–2 tbsp milk for brushing

For the dough: Mix soft butter and cream cheese with a hand mixer. Add both flours and salt and knead quickly into a smooth dough. Wrap in foil and chill for at least 2 hours.

Line a baking sheet with parchment paper. Preheat the oven to 180°C/160°C fan.

Halve the dough. Roll each portion out on a lightly floured surface into a 30-cm circle. Spread with pesto and sprinkle with Parmesan. Cut each circle into twelve "pie slices" and roll them from the outside in to form crescents. Place with the tip down on the baking sheet and brush with milk.

Bake in the preheated oven for 20-25 minutes until golden brown. Remove and let cool.

PREPARATION TIME: 30 minutes plus at least 2 hours chilling and 20–25 minutes baking

SAVOURY SAGE DIAMONDS

These pretty, cheesy, sage-scented crispy cookies are quickly cut into diamonds with a pastry wheel.

MAKES ABOUT 50 PIECES

50 g Emmental or Gruyère cheese
50 g Parmesan
approx. 15 sage leaves
125 g wheat flour (Type 405) plus extra for rolling
25 g polenta (cornmeal)
approx. ½ tsp salt
120 g cold butter
1 egg yolk for brushing
2 tbsp sesame seeds for sprinkling

Grate the cheeses finely, chop the sage finely. Mix the cheese, sage, flour, polenta, salt, cold butter in flakes, and 1–2 tablespoons of cold water in a bowl and quickly knead into a smooth dough. Cover and chill for 60 minutes.

Preheat the oven to 200°C/180°C fan. Line a baking sheet with parchment paper.

Roll out the dough on a floured surface to 5 mm thick, then cut or roll into 6-cm long diamonds and place on the sheet. Re-knead the remaining dough, roll out again, cut more diamonds. Mix the egg yolk with ½ tbsp water, brush the diamonds, sprinkle with sesame seeds. Bake in the preheated oven for about 8 minutes until golden yellow, then remove and let cool.

PREPARATION TIME: 35 minutes plus 60 minutes chilling and approx. 8 minutes baking

CRISPY BUCKWHEAT-RYE CRACKERS

These rustic crackers are great to snack on plain. Or spread with butter or cream cheese and top with fresh veggies like cucumber, radish, cherry tomatoes, or avocado. A few cracks of pepper, some herbs, cress, or sprouts – let your creativity go wild!

FOR 2 BAKING SHEETS, APPROX. 32 CRACKERS
VEGAN

250 ml milk or plant-based alternative
200 g medium-coarse wholemeal rye meal
250 g wholewheat flour
4 tbsp fine buckwheat flakes (20 g)
50 g soft butter or non-dairy alternative
1 heaped tsp salt
2 tsp sea salt flakes for sprinkling

Warm the milk slightly. Combine rye meal, wholewheat flour, and 2 tablespoons buckwheat flakes (10 g) in a bowl. Add the warm milk, butter flakes, and salt. Knead first with the dough hooks of a hand mixer, then with hands into a smooth dough. Let rest for 10 minutes.

Preheat the oven to 200°C/180°C fan. Halve the dough and roll out each portion on a sheet of parchment paper very thin to fit a baking tray (approx. 25 × 35 cm). Transfer to trays. Brush with water and sprinkle with the remaining buckwheat flakes and sea salt flakes.

Bake in the preheated oven for 25–30 minutes until crispy. Remove and let cool on a wire rack, then break into pieces.

PREPARATION TIME: 30 minutes plus 25-30 minutes baking

ONE POT

SOUPS AND PASTA, RICE AND VEGETABLE DISHES

LIGHT AND CREAMY, SPICY AND HEARTY

PASTA WITH GREEN SPELT BOLOGNESE

Carb lovers will be happy here – pasta with grains, imagine that! The Bolognese also tastes fantastic in a lasagne.

SERVES 6
VEGAN

125 g green spelt
1–1.2 litres vegetable broth
200 g carrots
½ leek
2 stalks celery (or 100 g celeriac)
150 g mushrooms
1 onion
2–3 cloves of garlic
3 tbsp olive oil
2 heaped tbsp tomato paste
100 ml dry red wine (optional)
400 g tinned chopped tomatoes
2 bay leaves
1 small sprig rosemary
Salt
Black pepper
½ bunch parsley
1–2 pinches smoked paprika
400 g long pasta (e.g. tagliatelle or spaghetti)
approx. 50 g Parmesan (piece) or non-dairy hard cheese

Lightly toast the green spelt in a pot over low to medium heat, stirring occasionally, until it darkens slightly and develops a nutty aroma (about 3–5 minutes). Add 500 ml vegetable broth, bring to a boil, let simmer for 5 minutes, then remove from the heat and let it soak with the lid on.

In the meantime, wash and dice the carrots. Clean the leek and celery, cut into small cubes. Clean and finely chop the mushrooms. Peel and finely dice the onion and garlic. Heat the olive oil in a wide pot, sauté the vegetables for about 5 minutes until they begin to brown.

Add tomato paste, sauté briefly, deglaze with red wine or water. Add soaked green spelt, chopped tomatoes, remaining broth, bay leaves, rosemary, salt, and pepper. Bring to a boil, then simmer for about 25 minutes, stirring occasionally. Add more broth if necessary.

Wash the parsley, shake dry, finely chop. Stir into the sauce and season to taste with salt, pepper, and smoked paprika.

Cook the pasta in plenty of salted water until al dente. Drain and serve with the green spelt Bolognese. Grate Parmesan over the top.

PREPARATION TIME: 40 minutes plus 25 minutes cooking

ROCKET SOUP WITH RED RICE AND GOAT CHEESE

Red rice is grown in the Camargue region of southern France and in Italy – please don't confuse it with long-grain red jasmine rice or red fermented rice from China! The red grains are unpolished, so this whole grain rice retains its colour even after cooking. Here, it not only brings a nutty flavour but also helps make the soup more filling.

SERVES 4
VEGAN

SOUP
1 onion
1–2 garlic cloves
40 g butter or non-dairy alternative
2 tsp fennel seeds
40 g flour (Type 405)
50 ml dry vermouth (e.g. Noilly Prat) or white wine, optional
250 ml milk or plant-based alternative
750 ml vegetable broth
freshly ground black pepper
freshly grated nutmeg
150 g soft goat cheese or non-dairy alternative
100 g rocket

ALSO
125 g red rice (e.g. from the Camargue)
Salt
1 tbsp butter or non-dairy alternative

Cook the rice according to the package instructions in salted water for 35–40 minutes over low to medium heat (if cooked too vigorously, the grains may burst).

Meanwhile, for the soup, peel and finely dice the onion and garlic. Heat the butter in a pot and sauté the onion and garlic until translucent. Finely crush the fennel seeds in a mortar and stir them in. Sprinkle the flour over the mixture and briefly sauté, then deglaze with vermouth (or wine or water). Gradually pour in the milk and vegetable broth while stirring, then season with salt, pepper, and nutmeg. Bring to a boil, then simmer over low heat for 10 minutes.

Cut 100 g of goat cheese into small pieces and stir it into the hot soup until melted.

Wash the rocket, spin dry, set aside a few pretty leaves, and roughly chop the rest. Add the chopped rocket to the soup and purée until smooth. Keep the soup warm with the lid on.

Drain the rice in a sieve. In a pan, heat some butter, then briefly sauté the rice and the reserved rocket leaves. Cut the remaining goat cheese into small pieces.

Ladle the soup into bowls, and top with the rocket-rice mixture and goat cheese.

PREPARATION TIME: 40 minutes

ROCKET PASTA

The rocket leaves rolled into the dough are not only visually striking, the noodles also taste wonderfully 'herb-green'.

SERVES 4

PASTA DOUGH
300 g flour (Tipo 00 / 'pizza flour')
3 eggs (size M)
1–2 tbsp lukewarm water
1 tbsp olive oil
1 tsp salt

2 cloves garlic
1 small chilli pepper
100 g rocket
2 tbsp pine nuts
2 tbsp olive oil
50 g Parmesan

For the pasta dough: Knead flour, eggs, 1–2 tablespoons lukewarm water, 1 tablespoon olive oil, and 1 teaspoon salt vigorously by hand for 5–10 minutes until you have a smooth, elastic dough. Wrap the dough in plastic wrap and let rest for 30 minutes at room temperature.

Meanwhile, peel and thinly slice the garlic. Seed the chilli and finely chop. Wash the rocket and dry thoroughly.

Halve the dough. Roll out the first portion using a pasta machine to the second-thinnest setting. Lay the sheet of dough on the work surface, cover half of it with a handful of rocket leaves, and fold the other half over it. Press the dough sheet gently with your hands so the rocket doesn't slip. Feed the folded sheet through the pasta machine again on a medium setting, then roll thinner step by step. Cut the pasta into thin strips. Repeat with the second half of the dough.

Heat the remaining olive oil in a pan. Add garlic, chilli, and pine nuts and lightly brown, then remove from heat. Finely grate the Parmesan.

Cook the pasta in plenty of salted water until al dente. Drain, reserving some cooking water. Return the pasta to the pot, add the remaining rocket, the pine nut mixture, and a little pasta water, and gently toss. Plate and sprinkle with grated Parmesan.

PREPARATION TIME: 60 minutes plus 30 minutes resting

RED PEPPER SOUP WITH POLENTA CROUTONS

Polenta here is not served as creamy mash, but as crispy fried croutons on a summery Mediterranean soup. You can also sprinkle the golden cubes over a salad.

SERVES 4
VEGAN

POLENTA CROUTONS
Salt
Black pepper
100 g polenta (instant)
1 tbsp olive oil for frying

SOUP
1 kg red peppers
1 large onion
2–3 cloves garlic
4 tbsp olive oil
2 tbsp tomato paste
½–1 tsp smoked paprika
2 tsp sweet paprika
2 tbsp balsamic vinegar
500 ml vegetable broth
500 ml strained tinned tomatoes
2 small sprigs rosemary
Salt
Black pepper

ALSO
2 tbsp high-quality olive oil for drizzling
2 tbsp basil leaves for garnish

For the polenta croutons: Bring 300 ml water, 2 pinches of salt, and a little pepper to a boil. Stir in the polenta with a whisk. Reduce heat and cook the polenta for about 3 minutes into a thick mash, stirring constantly with a wooden spoon. Remove from heat. Line a cutting board with parchment paper and spread the cornmeal mash finger-thick on top. Let the polenta cool for about 60 minutes.

For the soup: Deseed the peppers and cut into rough pieces. Peel and finely dice the onion and garlic cloves. Heat the olive oil in a pot and sauté the pepper pieces for about 8 minutes until they begin to brown. Add the onion and garlic and briefly sauté. Stir in tomato paste and both types of paprika powder, deglaze with balsamic vinegar. Then add the vegetable broth and strained tomatoes. Add rosemary and bring to a boil. Simmer covered for 15 minutes until the pepper pieces are soft.

Cut the cooled polenta into small cubes and fry in a pan with olive oil until crispy all over. Remove the rosemary from the soup, purée the soup finely and season to taste.

Divide the soup among bowls, top with croutons, drizzle with olive oil, and sprinkle with basil leaves.

PREPARATION TIME: 50 minutes plus 60 minutes cooling

MAKLOUBA WITH MINT YOGURT

Maklouba originates from Palestine. This rice dish is cooked on the stove and then flipped – hence its name Maklouba literally means 'upside down'.

SERVES 4

MAKLOUBA
300 g basmati rice
1 tsp ground turmeric
2–3 tsp Ras el-Hanout
1 tsp finely grated zest of an untreated lemon
Salt
Freshly ground black pepper
500 g aubergines
500 g tomatoes
2 green peppers
8–10 tbsp olive oil
600 ml strong vegetable broth
2 tbsp unpeeled almonds
2 tbsp pine nuts

MINT YOGURT
2 tbsp chopped mint leaves
500 g plain yogurt
2–3 splashes of lemon juice
Salt
Freshly ground black pepper

Mix the rice with turmeric, Ras el-Hanout, lemon zest, 1 heaped teaspoon of salt, and a little pepper.

Cut the aubergines and tomatoes into 1 cm thick slices. Core the peppers and cut into 2 cm wide strips. Sear the aubergines in batches in a pan with hot olive oil until soft and well browned. Remove and briefly sear the peppers in the remaining oil. Season the vegetables with salt and pepper.

Grease a rounded pot (about 22 cm in diameter) with some oil. Lay a layer of aubergine slices in the bottom, slightly overlapping. Then alternate layers of the remaining vegetables and rice, creating four to five layers total. Pour the vegetable broth over everything.

Cover the pot with a lid, bring to a boil, then reduce the heat and let the rice dish simmer gently for about 20 minutes.

Meanwhile, mix together the ingredients for the yogurt. Roughly chop the almonds and lightly toast them together with the pine nuts in a dry pan.

After 20 minutes, check if the liquid has been absorbed (if not, leave the pot on the switched-off stove for another 5–10 minutes).

Place a large plate over the pot and carefully flip the maklouba onto it. Sprinkle with the almonds and pine nuts. Serve with the mint yogurt.

PREPARATION TIME: 60 minutes plus 20 minutes cooking

GREEN SPELT RISOTTO WITH OVEN-ROASTED PUMPKIN

That pumpkin tastes especially good from the oven is now widely known, right? What I also wish would become known how delicious and flavourful a risotto made with green spelt is!

SERVES 4

VEGAN

1 onion
1 clove garlic
1½–2 l vegetable broth
3 tbsp olive oil
500 g green spelt
2 tbsp tomato paste
125 ml dry white wine
1 bay leaf
Salt
Freshly ground black pepper
1 kg Hokkaido pumpkin
2 tbsp maple syrup
1 tsp thyme leaves
50 g pumpkin seeds
100 g vegan cream cheese
2–3 tbsp lemon juice
2 tbsp fresh herbs (parsley, thyme, etc.)

Peel and finely dice the onion and garlic for the risotto. Heat the vegetable broth. Heat 1 tablespoon of olive oil in a pot and sauté the onion until translucent. Add garlic and briefly sauté. Add the green spelt and tomato paste and stir to combine. Deglaze with white wine and reduce briefly. Add a ladle of hot vegetable broth, the bay leaf, and some salt and pepper. Simmer the green spelt for 25–30 minutes until tender, gradually adding the remaining hot broth.

Meanwhile, preheat the oven to 220°C/200°C fan. Line a baking tray with parchment paper. Wash the pumpkin, remove seeds and fibres, and cut into about 1 cm thick wedges. Spread on the tray. Mix 2 tablespoons of olive oil, maple syrup, salt, pepper, and thyme and brush the pumpkin slices with it. Roast in the preheated oven for 15–20 minutes until well browned and roasted.

Toast the pumpkin seeds in a dry pan briefly and chop coarsely. When the green spelt is soft and the risotto nice and creamy, stir in the cream cheese and the roasted pumpkin wedges (they should fall apart slightly, which makes the risotto wonderfully creamy!). Season the risotto with salt, pepper, and lemon juice, and top with pumpkin seeds and herb leaves.

PREPARATION TIME: 60 minutes

SAVOY CABBAGE ROLLS WITH MILLET AND MUSTARD SAUCE

A feel-good meal par excellence are these savoury stuffed savoy cabbage rolls swimming in creamy mustard sauce.

SERVES 4

200 g millet
Salt
12 large savoy cabbage leaves
1 onion
1–2 cloves garlic
200 g carrots
100 g strong cheese or Emmental
1 bunch parsley
4–6 sprigs each thyme and oregano
1 egg (size M)
Black pepper, freshly ground
Freshly grated nutmeg
2 tbsp olive oil
500 ml vegetable broth
200 ml cream
2 tsp Dijon mustard
2–3 tsp whole grain mustard
2 tsp cornflour
Kitchen twine for tying

For the filling: Rinse the millet thoroughly in a fine sieve and let drain. Then cook in a covered pot with 400 ml salted water for 8 minutes. Remove from heat, let sit covered for a few minutes, and transfer to a bowl.

Meanwhile, trim the thick centre ribs from the savoy cabbage leaves. Blanch the leaves in boiling salted water for 3–4 minutes, then remove, drain in a sieve, rinse with cold water, and pat dry or allow to drain well. Lay out flat on the work surface.

Peel and finely dice the onion and garlic. Peel and coarsely grate the carrots; coarsely grate the cheese. Rinse the herbs, shake dry, remove thin stems and finely chop leaves. Mix onion, garlic, carrots, cheese, egg, and herbs into the millet. Season well with salt, pepper, and nutmeg.

Place 1½ heaped tablespoons of filling on each cabbage leaf. Fold the sides inward and roll up tightly. Tie with kitchen twine.

Heat the olive oil in a large roasting pan or pot and sear the cabbage rolls on all sides (possibly in batches) until lightly browned. Pour in the vegetable broth, bring to a boil, and let simmer covered for 15 minutes.

Remove the rolls, stir the cream and both types of mustard into the sauce. Mix the cornflour with 2–3 tablespoons cold water and use to thicken the sauce. Season with salt and pepper. Serve the cabbage rolls with the sauce.

PREPARATION TIME: 60 minutes plus 15 minutes cooking

BARLEY RISOTTO WITH OVEN-ROASTED CHERRY TOMATOES AND GORGONZOLA

What do I love about a barley risotto? The taste, of course! But also that barley forgives me a few extra minutes of cooking time and still keeps its bite. Even when reheated, a barley risotto never turns mushy like rice risotto. I cook this risotto in midsummer, when aromatic cherry tomatoes are abundant.

SERVES 4

VEGAN

OVEN-ROASTED TOMATOES

1 kg cherry tomatoes
1 tbsp sugar
Salt
Freshly ground black pepper

RISOTTO

1 onion
2 cloves garlic
2 tbsp butter or non-dairy alternative
2 heaping tbsp tomato paste
100 ml white wine (optional)
375 g pearl barley
1 bay leaf
1–1.2 l vegetable broth
3–4 tsp lemon juice
Salt
Freshly ground black pepper

ALSO

125 g Gorgonzola or non-dairy alternative
2 tbsp marjoram leaves for garnish

Preheat the oven to 160°C/140°C fan. Halve the cherry tomatoes. Line a baking tray with parchment paper and arrange the tomatoes cut side up. Sprinkle with sugar, 1 teaspoon of salt, and plenty of pepper. Bake in the preheated oven for 45–60 minutes, briefly opening the oven door two to three times during baking to let steam escape. The tomatoes should remain slightly soft, not completely dried.

For the risotto: Peel and finely dice the onion and garlic. Sauté in butter until translucent. Add tomato paste and briefly roast, then deglaze with white wine (or water) and let reduce slightly. Add the barley and bay leaf, pour in vegetable broth, and bring to a boil.

Simmer over low heat for about 20 minutes, stirring occasionally, until the barley is done and the risotto is creamy-soupy. Add more broth if needed. Remove the bay leaf, stir in half of the oven-roasted tomatoes. Season with lemon juice, salt, and pepper.

Divide the risotto onto plates, portion the Gorgonzola into four pieces and place on top with the remaining tomatoes. Sprinkle with marjoram leaves.

PREPARATION TIME: 40 minutes plus 45–60 minutes roasting

PASTA IN BROTH WITH HERB AND RICOTTA FILLING

When I want to really spoil my family, I make this soup. The reward for kneading, rolling out, and filling a thoroughly delicious meal.

SERVES 4

PASTA DOUGH

150 g flour (Tipo 00 or Type 405), plus extra for dusting
25 g fine semolina (durum wheat)
1 egg (size M)
1 egg yolk (size M)
2 tsp olive oil
½ tsp salt
A pinch of ground turmeric

FILLING

1 onion
1 clove of garlic
1 tbsp butter
75 g mixed herbs (e.g. basil, parsley, oregano)
75 g strong cheese
250 g ricotta
1½ tsp finely grated zest of an untreated lemon
4–5 tbsp breadcrumbs
2 egg yolks (size M)
Salt, freshly ground black pepper, nutmeg

ALSO

1.5 litres good, strong vegetable broth
2 tbsp finely chopped chives

For the pasta dough: Knead the flour, semolina, egg, egg yolk, olive oil, salt, and turmeric vigorously by hand for 5–10 minutes until smooth and elastic. Wrap the dough in plastic wrap and let rest for 30 minutes at room temperature.

Meanwhile, for the filling, peel and finely dice the onion and garlic. Sauté in butter until translucent and transfer to a bowl.

Rinse the herbs, shake dry, and finely chop. Grate the cheese finely. Add herbs, cheese, ricotta, lemon zest, breadcrumbs, and egg yolks to the onion mixture. Mix thoroughly and season well with salt, pepper, and nutmeg.

Briefly knead the rested pasta dough and roll out using a pasta machine. Brush the top long edge lightly with water. Spread the filling thinly over the dough, leaving a narrow border. Fold the dough from bottom to top and press down gently. Use the handle of a wooden spoon to press the dough into segments about 5 cm apart. Cut into individual pieces.

Bring plenty of salted water to a boil in a large pot. Drop in the filled pasta. Once they float to the surface, reduce the heat and let simmer gently for about 8 minutes.

Heat the vegetable broth. Divide the filled pasta among plates, ladle the broth over them, and sprinkle with chives.

PREPARATION TIME: 1½ hours plus 30 minutes resting

AUTHENTIC ITALIAN PASTA

Durum wheat semolina, water, and salt – these are the ingredients for the pasta dough Maria makes fresh twice a day. Once early in the morning for lunch, when the hungry office crowd from the nearby buildings looks forward to a plate of pasta, and once again in the afternoon for the evening guests.

The sack of finely ground semolina, *semola di grano duro*, stored under the worktable, naturally comes from Italy. After all, the small pasta restaurant is called *Jill's pasta autentica*.

But the boss of the pasta is not Jill – it's Maria. Maria is from Naples, where she learned how to make pasta. As a child, from her aunt, she says with a deep laugh: 'Back then a tedious chore, today I say *mille grazie, zia*, for the early training.'

For twenty minutes, the dough ingredients are kneaded in the stainless-steel commercial mixer until the dough is elastic and passes Maria's critical eye and touch. Even though there's a recipe, the amount of water always varies slightly – every sack of *semola di grano duro* is different, and even the humidity in the air affects the dough's consistency.

Italian durum wheat has a high protein (gluten) content, which gives the dough a firm texture and makes it ideal for pasta making. No eggs go into the dough for what's called *pasta secca*, as egg pasta (*pasta all'uovo*) is more common in Northern Italy.

Once Maria is satisfied with the dough, she feeds it in portions into the pasta machine, which rolls it out into long sheets and then cuts them into narrow tagliatelle or very fine tagliolini. With practised movements, Maria dusts the fresh noodles with a little semola and hangs them over a thin rod to dry.

For ravioli, the dough sheets are rolled out even thinner and punched into rounds by hand. '*Fatto a mano*, handmade – that's why they're so expensive,' says Maria with another deep laugh. For square ravioli, she pulls a *tagliapasta* from a drawer under the worktable. What's the English word for this tool that cuts pasta into exact rectangles or squares? '*Tagliapasta*,' she shrugs, continuing to cut with calm, skilled motions.

Even the filling is prepared entirely by hand. Using a piping bag, Maria places the filling in the centre of each pasta round, brushes the edges with a little water, and folds the dough neatly over the filling. Do I need to ask if she also makes the fillings and sauces herself? Probably not. Because the boss of the pasta is – of course – Maria!

BIBIMBAP WITH RADISH PICKLES

I like to call the rice bowl the 'mother of all bowls', because Bibimbap is not a new trend but a truly 'old hat' in Korean cuisine. Without the garlicky and chilli-spicy Gochujang sauce, this delicious rice dish would not be complete. Take my toppings as a suggestion and let your imagination run wild!

SERVES 4

VEGAN

RADISH PICKLES

½ bunch radishes
20 g fresh ginger
100 ml white wine vinegar
3 tbsp sugar
2 tsp salt

TOFU

300 g plain tofu
15 g fresh ginger
2 cloves garlic
3 tbsp light soy sauce
1 tbsp Gochujang (Korean chilli paste)
1 tbsp sugar

GOCHUJANG SAUCE

4–8 cloves garlic
2 heaped tbsp Gochujang
4 tbsp soy sauce
2 tbsp rice vinegar
Salt, freshly ground black pepper

For the radish pickles: Trim the radishes and slice thinly. Peel and finely chop the ginger. Bring vinegar, 150 ml water, ginger, sugar, and 2 teaspoons of salt to a boil, pour hot over the radishes, let cool, and marinate for at least 2 hours.

Pat the tofu dry and cut into cubes. Peel and finely chop the ginger and garlic, mix with soy sauce, Gochujang paste, and sugar, then toss with the tofu. Marinate for at least 2 hours.

Meanwhile, cook the rice. Soak the rice in cold water, rinse in the soaking water, drain in a sieve, and rinse again with fresh water. Repeat until the water runs clear. Drain again, return to the pot, cover with 850 ml fresh, lightly salted water. Bring to a boil, then simmer covered over low heat for about 15 minutes. Remove from heat and let sit for 5 minutes. Keep the rice covered and warm.

For the Gochujang sauce: Peel and finely chop the garlic. Mix with Gochujang paste, soy sauce, vinegar, and 3–4 tablespoons water. Season with salt and pepper – caution, the sauce is very spicy!

For the vegetables: Trim the pointed cabbage, peel the carrots, and cut both into thin strips. Halve the pak choi lengthwise and trim the ends. Remove the stems from the shiitake mushrooms and halve the caps.

ALSO

400 g sushi rice
Salt
200 g pointed cabbage
200 g carrots
250 g mini pak choi
200 g shiitake mushrooms
4 tbsp vegetable oil
1 tbsp toasted sesame oil
Freshly ground black pepper
2 tbsp soy sauce
2 tbsp cress for garnish

Heat 1 tbsp vegetable oil and sesame oil in a pan. Briefly sauté the pak choi, remove. Then sauté the cabbage and carrots briefly and intensely, season with salt and pepper, and remove. Heat 1 tbsp oil and sauté the shiitake briefly and intensely, deglaze with soy sauce and set aside. Sauté the tofu cubes along with the marinade in the remaining oil.

To serve, fluff up the rice and divide among bowls. Arrange tofu, vegetables, shiitake, and drained radish pickles on top and drizzle with Gochujang sauce.

Traditionally, the rice is well mixed with all 'toppings' before eating – using a spoon.

PREPARATION TIME: 1½ hours plus 2 hours marinating

HAZELNUT POLENTA WITH BRAISED RED CABBAGE AND BROWN BUTTER

I'm always surprised how a little hazelnut flour transforms the flavour of polenta. Combined with savoury red cabbage and the hazelnut-sage butter, this meal is one of my winter favourites.

SERVES 4
VEGAN

RED CABBAGE

1 onion
1 kg red cabbage
3 tbsp butter or non-dairy alternative
75 ml balsamic vinegar
75 ml red wine vinegar
500 ml apple juice
Salt
2 cinnamon sticks
2 bay leaves
10 allspice berries
5 cloves
1 large tart apple
1 tsp grated zest of an untreated orange
200 g elderberry or red currant jelly
2–3 tsp cornflour
Freshly ground black pepper

HAZELNUT POLENTA

50 g ground hazelnuts
500 ml milk or plant-based alternative
1 bay leaf
2 tbsp butter or non-dairy alternative
Salt, freshly ground black pepper
Freshly grated nutmeg
150 g polenta (instant)

For the red cabbage: Peel and finely dice the onion. Remove the outer leaves from the red cabbage, quarter and core it. Slice the cabbage into fine strips. Heat the butter in a large pot and sauté the onion until translucent. Add the red cabbage and sauté for about 5 minutes, stirring. Deglaze with balsamic and red wine vinegar, pour in apple juice, and add a little salt. Add just enough water to cover the cabbage and bring to a boil. Braise covered over medium heat for a total of 90 minutes, stirring occasionally and adding more water if needed.

Finely crush the spices in a mortar. Peel, quarter, core the apple, and slice it. Add orange zest, crushed spices, apple slices, and jelly to the cabbage. Boil uncovered for another 20–30 minutes until most of the liquid evaporates.

Dissolve the cornflour in 2 tablespoons cold water and stir into the cabbage to slightly thicken. Season with salt and pepper.

Briefly toast ground hazelnuts in a pot while stirring until fragrant. Add milk, 250 ml water, bay leaf, and butter, and bring to a boil. Season with salt, pepper, and nutmeg. Stir in the polenta and cook for 1–2 minutes while stirring. Remove from heat, cover, and let it swell for 5–10 minutes.

HAZELNUT-SAGE BUTTER

60 g hazelnut flakes
80 g butter or non-dairy alternative
15–20 sage leaves

Briefly toast hazelnut flakes in a pan. Add the butter and heat until lightly browned and nutty-smelling. Add the sage leaves and fry until crispy.

To serve spoon red cabbage and polenta onto plates and drizzle with hazelnut-sage butter.

PREPARATION TIME: 50 minutes plus 90 minutes braising (red cabbage)

BLACK VENERE RICE RISOTTO WITH SPINACH

Black rice has been cultivated in China for centuries and now also grows in Piedmont. The round grains are not hulled, which keeps them black during cooking but also means they take much longer to soften than white risotto rice.

SERVES 4

VEGAN

RISOTTO

1 onion
1–2 cloves garlic
approx. 1.5 litres vegetable broth
2 tbsp butter or non-dairy alternative
250 g black Venere rice
2 bay leaves
3–4 sprigs thyme
100 ml white wine
Salt
Freshly ground black pepper
Freshly grated nutmeg

ALSO

800 g leaf spinach
1 onion
1 clove garlic
1–2 tbsp butter or non-dairy alternative
250 g crème fraîche or plant-based alternative
2 tsp grated zest of an untreated lemon
Salt
Freshly ground black pepper

For the risotto: Peel and finely dice the onion and garlic. Bring the vegetable broth to a boil. In a pot, melt the butter and sauté the onion until translucent. Stir in the garlic and sauté briefly. Add the rice, bay leaves, and thyme and deglaze with white wine. Add a ladle of hot vegetable broth and stir. Let simmer uncovered until almost all the broth is absorbed, then add more broth gradually. Cook the risotto for 45-60 minutes in total. By the end, the rice grains should still have a bit of bite. Season with salt, pepper, and nutmeg.

Meanwhile, wash and drain the spinach. Peel and finely dice the onion and garlic. Heat a large pot, add the damp spinach, and let it wilt. Drain in a sieve, rinse with cold water, and drain thoroughly.

Wipe out the pot, add butter, and sauté the diced onion until translucent. Add garlic and briefly sauté. Stir in the spinach and crème fraîche and heat briefly. Season with 1 tsp lemon zest, salt, and pepper.

Once the risotto is done, remove the thyme and bay leaves. Stir the spinach mixture into the rice and serve on (preferably warmed) plates. Sprinkle with the remaining lemon zest.

PREPARATION TIME: 30 minutes plus 45–60 minutes cooking

HEARTY EINKORN VEGETABLE STEW

Einkorn is one of the most ancient cultivated grains, along with emmer. It is nutritionally valuable, well-tolerated, and making a comeback. Its slightly yellow colour also makes baked goods beautiful – but these healthy grains also shine in dishes like this hearty stew.

SERVES 4
VEGAN

125 g einkorn (or wheat or spelt)
1 onion
1 clove garlic
1 thin leek stalk
2 stalks celery
250 g carrots
1 small kohlrabi
1 tbsp butter or non-dairy alternative
approx. 1¼ l vegetable broth
3 sprigs thyme
Salt
Freshly ground black pepper
Freshly grated nutmeg
150 g hard cheese or non-dairy alternative)
200 g crème fraîche or plant-based alternative

Soak the einkorn in cold water the night before. The next day, drain in a sieve, rinse with cold water, and let drip off.

Peel and finely dice the onion and garlic. Clean, peel, or scrub the remaining vegetables well. Slice the leek and celery thinly, and dice the carrots and kohlrabi small. Heat the butter in a pot, sauté the onion and garlic. Add the vegetables and einkorn, pour in the broth and add thyme. Season with salt, pepper, and nutmeg and bring to a boil. Simmer over low heat for 15–20 minutes until the grain and vegetables are tender.

Grate the cheese finely. Stir in the cheese and crème fraîche and briefly bring to a boil. Season the stew with salt, pepper, and nutmeg.

PREPARATION TIME: 25 minutes plus overnight soaking and 15–20 minutes cooking

SWEETS

CRISPY YEAST WAFFLES

Einkorn, like emmer and kamut, is one of the ancient grains. There is only one grain on each notch of the ear's spindle, hence its name. To bake bread with it, einkorn flour should be mixed with flour rich in gluten. But for these airy waffles, the healthy, protein-rich einkorn flour alone is sufficient. You can also use wheat or spelt flour instead.

MAKES 12-14 PIECES

300 ml milk
500 g wholemeal einkorn flour
½ cube fresh yeast
150 g butter
125 g sugar
3 eggs (size M)
¼ tsp salt
Vegetable oil for greasing the waffle iron
Powdered sugar for dusting

EQUIPMENT
Waffle iron

Gently heat the milk until lukewarm. Put the flour into a bowl and make a well in the centre. Crumble in the yeast, pour in the milk, and stir with a bit of flour from the edge. Cover and let this pre-dough rise in a warm place for 15 minutes.

Melt the butter in a small saucepan and let it cool until lukewarm. Add sugar, eggs, lukewarm butter, and salt to the risen pre-dough and knead vigorously for about 5 minutes using the dough hooks of a hand mixer. The dough will be quite sticky. Cover the bowl again and let the dough rise for about 45 minutes until doubled in size.

Preheat a square "Brussels" waffle iron and lightly grease the baking surfaces with oil. For each waffle, place 1 heaping tablespoon of dough in the centre of the waffle iron, then close it. Bake the waffles until golden brown, remove, and let steam briefly on a wire rack. Repeat until all waffles are baked. Dust with powdered sugar.

PREPARATION TIME: 25 minutes plus approx. 60 minutes for rising and baking

EMMER PANCAKES WITH PLUMS

When you eat these delicious pancakes – early in the morning, for a late breakfast, lunch, or with afternoon coffee – I'll leave that up to you. I think they taste great anytime.

SERVES 4

PANCAKE BATTER

125 g wholemeal emmer flour
1 tbsp sugar
1 tsp baking powder
1 generous pinch of salt
200 ml milk
2 eggs (size M)

ALSO

4 tbsp walnut kernels
8–10 plums
approx. 2 tbsp butter for frying
4 tbsp emmer or oat flakes
4–6 tbsp cream yogurt
Some ground cinnamon
4 tbsp maple syrup for drizzling

For the pancake batter: Mix emmer flour, sugar, baking powder, and salt in a bowl. Whisk together milk, 500 ml cold water, and the eggs, then stir into the flour mixture until smooth. Let the batter rest for 15 minutes.

Meanwhile, roughly chop the walnuts. Pit the plums and cut into thin wedges.

Heat some butter in a non-stick pan. For each pancake, pour a quarter of the batter into the pan, distribute a few plum wedges, the walnuts, and the emmer or oat flakes over it. Cook the pancake for 1–2 minutes, then flip and cook the second side until golden. Repeat to make all the pancakes.

Serve the pancakes with yogurt, cinnamon, and a drizzle of maple syrup.

PREPARATION TIME: 30 minutes plus 15 minutes resting

FRUITY MILLET-ALMOND BALLS

First one, then two ... and suddenly the tin is empty – these fruity, juicy balls disappear into mouths so quickly. If that isn't a compliment, I don't know what is!

MAKES 20 PIECES
VEGAN

- 75 g unblanched almonds
- 50 g millet flakes
- 100 g dried figs
- 100 g dried mango
- 2 tbsp unhulled sesame seeds
- 1½ tbsp cocoa powder
- 1 tsp ground cinnamon
- 3 tbsp white or brown almond butter
- 2 tbsp agave syrup

Roughly chop the almonds, then toast with the millet flakes in a dry pan until fragrant and slightly browned. Let cool, transfer to a food processor, and grind finely. Set aside 2 tablespoons of this mixture in a shallow dish.

Add figs, mango, sesame seeds, cocoa powder, and cinnamon to the food processor and mix everything finely. Knead in the almond butter and agave syrup. Form the mixture into balls about 3 cm in size.

Roll the balls in the reserved almond-millet mixture. They will keep in an airtight container for 1-2 weeks.

PREPARATION TIME: 30 minutes

HEARTY GRANOLA BARS WITH DATES

I'm not a fan of store-bought granola bars, but these are a loyal companion on hikes. They're packed with healthy ingredients, not too sweet, but also don't taste 'too healthy' and are wonderfully crispy!

MAKES 12 PIECES
VEGAN

200 g dried dates
100 g hazelnuts
50 g pumpkin seeds
50 g sunflower seeds
1 tbsp flaxseed
1 tbsp sesame seeds
200 g coarse rolled oats
2 tsp ground cinnamon
1 pinch of salt
125 g liquid honey or maple syrup
4 tbsp vegetable oil

Pour 100 ml of hot water over the dates and let them soak for 30 minutes. Then purée them in a blender together with the soaking water to form a paste.

Chop the hazelnuts. Mix with pumpkin and sunflower seeds, flaxseed, sesame, oats, cinnamon, and salt. Stir the date purée together with the honey or maple syrup and oil, then thoroughly combine with the dry ingredients.

Preheat the oven to 180°C/160°C fan. Line a small baking tray or baking dish (approx. 22 × 30 cm) with parchment paper. Spread the mixture 1–1½ cm thick on the tray and smooth it out. Bake in the centre of the oven for about 30 minutes until golden brown.

Lift the baked mixture out of the tray using the parchment paper, place on a wire rack, and allow to cool until lukewarm. Then cut into bars on a chopping board and let cool completely.

PREPARATION TIME: 15 minutes plus 30 minutes soaking and approx. 30 minutes baking

ONE PAN

CRISPY DISHES FROM THE PAN

FRIED AND ROASTED, STIR-FRIED AND SIZZLED

GREEN SPELT-SPINACH PATTIES

These savoury green spelt patties win over even the most devoted meat-eaters with their hearty flavour – and they're also great served in burger buns (p. 134). Cracked green spelt can be purchased pre-ground in supermarkets or health food stores. You can use any leftovers to make green spelt Bolognese (p. 64) or green spelt balls (p. 160).

SERVES 4
VEGAN

200 g cracked green spelt
600 ml vegetable broth
200 g fine spinach or baby spinach
1 onion
approx. 6 tbsp vegetable oil for frying
1 bunch parsley
4–5 tbsp breadcrumbs
2 tsp Dijon mustard
2 tbsp soy sauce
Salt
Freshly ground black pepper
Freshly grated nutmeg

Bring the cracked green spelt to a boil in the vegetable broth in a saucepan, then simmer covered on low heat for 15 minutes, stirring frequently. Let it continue to swell on the switched-off stove for another 10 minutes. Remove the pot from the stove and let the green spelt cool completely.

Wash the spinach, drain well, and coarsely chop. Peel and finely dice the onion. Sauté the onion in 1 tablespoon vegetable oil until translucent. Add the spinach and let it wilt briefly, then remove from the heat. Rinse the parsley, shake dry, remove thin stems and finely chop the leaves.

In a bowl, mix the onion-spinach mixture, parsley, green spelt, breadcrumbs, mustard, and soy sauce. Season generously with salt, pepper, and nutmeg. Let the mixture rest for 10 minutes.

Heat some vegetable oil in a wide frying pan. With damp hands, form about twelve patties from the mixture and fry them in batches over medium heat for 6–8 minutes on each side until golden brown. Drain on paper towels.

PREPARATION TIME: 30 minutes plus 25 minutes cooking and swelling

CHANTERELLE PANCAKES WITH PUMPKIN SEED CREAM

I'm not that fond of sweet pancakes, but I'll gladly help myself to a second serving of this savoury version. Perhaps that has something to do with the delicious chanterelles.

SERVES 4

PUMPKIN SEED CREAM
2 tbsp pumpkin seeds
250 g sour cream or crème fraîche
2 tbsp pumpkin seed oil
Salt, freshly ground black pepper
½ bunch chives

PANCAKES
300 g small chanterelles
1 shallot
½ bunch parsley
50 g Parmesan (block)
4 eggs (size M)
350 ml milk
250 g spelt flour (Type 630)
Salt
Freshly ground black pepper
1–2 tbsp vegetable oil and butter each for frying

For the pumpkin seed cream: Toast the pumpkin seeds in a pan without fat until lightly browned. Let cool and chop finely. Mix the sour cream, pumpkin seed oil, and pumpkin seeds. Season with salt and pepper. Rinse the chives, shake dry, cut into fine rings, and sprinkle over the cream. Set aside.

For the pancakes: Clean the chanterelles thoroughly with a brush, trimming off any bad spots. Leave small mushrooms whole and cut larger ones into pieces. Peel and finely dice the shallot. Wash the parsley, shake dry, pluck the leaves, and coarsely chop them.

Grate the Parmesan. Separate the eggs. Mix the milk, egg yolks, and flour vigorously with a whisk until smooth and lump-free. Season with salt and pepper. Beat the egg whites until stiff and fold into the batter.

In two large pans, heat a little oil and butter. Sauté the chanterelles and shallot over medium heat until lightly browned. Season with salt and pepper, stir in the parsley.

Pour half of the batter over the mushrooms in each pan. Leave to set over medium heat. After 3-4 minutes, divide into quarters with a spatula, flip, and cook the second side for another 4 minutes. Break the pancakes into pieces and serve with the pumpkin seed cream.

PREPARATION TIME: 35 minutes

KANTINE

MILLET PATTIES WITH POTATO SALAD

Patties, burgers – whatever you call them these disappear in no time. And the same goes for the potato salad.

SERVES 4

VEGAN

POTATO SALAD

1 kg small waxy potatoes
1 onion
200 ml strong vegetable broth
4 tbsp red wine vinegar
1–2 tsp Dijon mustard
Salt
Freshly ground black pepper
5 tbsp vegetable oil
2 tbsp chopped chives

PATTIES

150 g millet
Salt
70 g ground flaxseed
1 large carrot
½ bunch spring onions
3–4 sprigs each marjoram and parsley
2 tsp whole grain mustard
Freshly ground black pepper
2–3 tbsp olive oil for frying

For the potato salad: Wash the potatoes, cover with water in a pot, and cook for just under 20 minutes until done. Drain, rinse briefly with cold water, and let cool slightly. Peel and finely dice the onion, bring to a boil with the broth, then remove from heat. Stir in vinegar and mustard.

Peel the potatoes, slice thinly, and place in a wide bowl. Pour the hot onion broth over them, season with salt and pepper, and gently mix. Let sit covered for about 30 minutes, then stir in the oil. Season to taste again if needed.

For the patties: Rinse the millet thoroughly in a sieve and drain. Cook in 600 ml salted water for 12 minutes. Remove from heat, stir in the flaxseed, and let swell covered for about 10 minutes.

Scrub or peel the carrot, then grate finely. Trim and finely slice the spring onions. Rinse the herbs, shake dry, strip the tender stems and finely chop the leaves. Mix carrot, scallions, herbs, and mustard with the millet mixture and season generously with salt and pepper.

With damp hands, shape about eight patties from the millet mixture. Heat the oil in a large frying pan and fry the patties on both sides over medium-low heat until golden brown. Serve with the potato salad and sprinkle with chives.

PREPARATION TIME: 60 minutes plus 30 minutes resting

GREEN VEGETABLE PAELLA

I'm not really into grilling, but I love preparing this paella outside in the garden on the fire drum. As an aperitif beforehand, there's fresh bread with artichoke cream, and a glass of Cava is also welcome – a lovely meal for a sociable evening with friends!

SERVES 4

VEGAN

1 onion
2 cloves garlic
1–1¼ l vegetable broth
3 tbsp olive oil
2 tbsp tomato paste
2 tsp sweet paprika
2 tsp hot paprika
approx. 1 tsp smoked paprika
0.1 g saffron threads
250 g paella rice (*arroz bomba*)
Salt
Freshly ground black pepper
150 g broad beans (fresh or frozen)
1 green pepper
250 g green beans
2–3 sprigs parsley

Peel and finely dice the onion and garlic. Heat the vegetable broth. In a wide pan, heat the olive oil and sauté the diced onion until golden yellow. Add garlic and briefly sauté. Stir in tomato paste, all of the paprika, saffron, and the rice. Pour in 1 litre of vegetable broth, season generously with salt and pepper, and bring to a boil. Let simmer gently over low heat for 15 minutes, until the liquid is almost completely absorbed.

Meanwhile, cook the broad beans in boiling salted water for 2 minutes, drain in a sieve, rinse with cold water, and squeeze the beans out of their skins. Halve and deseed the green pepper, then slice into strips. Trim and halve the green beans.

Add the pepper and green beans to the rice, stir, and cook for another 5 minutes. Then add the broad beans and simmer everything for 5 more minutes, until the rice and vegetables are cooked through. Add more vegetable broth if needed.

Wash and dry the parsley, pluck off the leaves, roughly chop, and sprinkle over the paella.

PREPARATION TIME: 40 minutes

BUCKWHEAT BLINI WITH DILL CREAM, RADISHES, AND TOASTED BUCKWHEAT

I like to serve these little buckwheat blinis as an aperitif. Aside from tasting great, they are so handy and pretty to look at.

FOR 4-6 PEOPLE MAKES 30 PIECES

BLINI
200 g buckwheat flour
Salt
1 tsp liquid honey
15 g fresh yeast
1 egg (size M)
2–3 tbsp vegetable oil for frying

TOPPING
2 tbsp whole buckwheat kernels
2 tbsp dill tips
200 g sour cream
Salt, freshly ground black pepper
½ bunch radishes
1½ tbsp white wine vinegar
2 tbsp vegetable oil
1 tbsp fennel blossoms, for garnish

For the blini: Mix the flour with a pinch of salt in a bowl. Stir 250 ml lukewarm water with the honey and yeast until smooth. Separate the egg. Add the yeast mixture and the egg yolk to the flour and beat with a hand mixer into a thick batter. Cover and let rise for about 45 minutes.

Meanwhile, toast the buckwheat kernels in a pan over low heat for 3-5 minutes until golden brown, then let cool.

Finely chop the dill and mix with the sour cream, adding some salt and pepper. Trim the radishes and slice thinly. Mix with vinegar, vegetable oil, a little salt, and pepper, and let sit briefly.

Briefly stir the batter. Beat the egg white until stiff and fold in. Heat a non-stick pan and brush lightly with oil. Bake about 30 blini one after another over medium heat. Drain on paper towels.

To serve, place a small dollop of dill cream and a few radish slices on each blini, and sprinkle with toasted buckwheat kernels and torn fennel blossoms.

PREPARATION TIME: 50 minutes plus 45 minutes resting

CHEESE-SPINACH SPAETZLE WITH CRISPY ONIONS

With a spaetzle press or spaetzle slicer, these spaetzle are quick to make and taste far better than shop-bought ones. The key to their flavour is the cheese – it has to be a strong, traditional mountain cheese!

SERVES 4

SPAETZLE DOUGH
400 g wheat flour (Type 405) or spelt flour (Type 630) + 3 tbsp flour
4 eggs (size M)
Salt
1 tbsp vegetable oil

500 g spinach
4 onions
5 tbsp butter
200-250 g strong cheese
Black pepper from the mill
1-2 pinches freshly grated nutmeg

For the spaetzle dough: Place the flour, eggs, 1½ tsp salt, vegetable oil, and about 125 ml water into a bowl. First mix well with the dough hooks of a hand mixer, then beat vigorously with a wooden spoon for about 5 minutes until the dough is smooth and forms bubbles. Let the dough rest for 15 minutes.

In a large pot, bring plenty of salted water to a boil. Working in batches, press the dough through a spaetzle press or slicer into the boiling water. As soon as the spaetzle rise to the surface, let them boil once, then remove with a slotted spoon, place in a sieve, rinse under cold water, and drain well.

Meanwhile, wash the spinach, drain thoroughly, and coarsely chop. Peel the onions and cut into fine rings, mix with 3 tbsp flour, then slowly fry in 3 tbsp butter over medium heat for 7–10 minutes until golden brown and crispy. Set aside.

Grate the cheese. Heat 2 tbsp butter in a wide pan, add the spaetzle, and fry without browning. Stir in the spinach and cheese and heat until the cheese has melted and the spinach is wilted. Season with salt, pepper, and nutmeg. Serve the spaetzle topped with the crispy onions.

PREPARATION TIME: 30 minutes plus 15 minutes resting

LA MENAGÈRE

SAVOURY SEMOLINA AND CHEESE SLICES WITH GARDEN SALSA

As a child I loved sweet semolina slices – who wouldn't, with lots of cinnamon and sugar? My grown-up, savoury version is served with a 'garden salsa' of tomatoes, cucumber, radishes, and spring onions.

SERVES 4

SEMOLINA SLICES

1 litre milk
2 tbsp butter
Salt
Black pepper from the mill
Freshly grated nutmeg
125 g strong mountain cheese or Emmental
3–4 sprigs each of sage and basil
250 g durum wheat semolina
4 eggs (size M)
approx. 75 g breadcrumbs for breading
2 tbsp butter and vegetable oil each for frying

GARDEN SALSA

1 mini cucumber
200 g cherry tomatoes
2 spring onions
6 radishes
3 tbsp lemon juice
4 tbsp olive oil
2 tbsp herb leaves
Salt
Freshly ground black pepper

For the semolina slices: Bring the milk to a boil with the butter, some salt, pepper, and nutmeg. Finely grate the cheese. Wash the herbs, shake dry, pluck the leaves, and finely chop. Stir the semolina and cheese into the milk. Let simmer while stirring constantly over low heat for 5 minutes to form a thick porridge. Remove from the heat, stir in 2 eggs and the herbs thoroughly.

Line a baking tray with parchment paper. Spread the semolina porridge finger-thick into a rectangle and let cool for about 30 minutes. Cut the cooled semolina into diamond shapes.

For breading: Beat the remaining 2 eggs in a deep plate. Place the breadcrumbs in a second plate. First dip the semolina slices in egg, then coat with breadcrumbs. Heat some butter and oil in a large frying pan and fry the semolina slices in batches for 3–4 minutes on each side until golden brown.

For the garden salsa: Clean the vegetables. Halve the cucumber and tomatoes and slice thinly. Cut the spring onions into thin rings and the radishes into thin slices. Mix with lemon juice, olive oil, herb leaves, some salt, and pepper. Let sit briefly and drizzle over the semolina slices.

PREPARATION TIME: 40 minutes plus 30 minutes cooling

EINKORN PANCAKES WITH SPINACH FILLING

The einkorn flour gives these vegan pancakes not only a mildly nutty flavour but also a golden-yellow colour. The binding comes from soy flour. So simple, so delicious!

SERVES 3–4

VEGAN

BATTER

375 g wholegrain einkorn flour (or wholewheat or spelt flour)
3 tbsp soy flour
2 tsp baking powder
Salt
4 tbsp olive oil
750 ml cold water

FILLING

1 kg spinach
Salt
1 untreated lemon
1 onion
1–2 garlic cloves
2 tbsp olive oil
250 g vegan cream cheese
Freshly ground black pepper

TO SERVE

1 tsp chilli flakes
2 tbsp sesame seeds

For the batter: Mix the einkorn flour, soy flour, baking powder, a pinch of salt, 2 tbsp olive oil, and the water with a whisk until smooth. Let the batter sit, covered, for 15 minutes.

Meanwhile, wash the spinach and allow it to drain. Blanch the spinach briefly in boiling salted water, drain in a colander, rinse with cold water, and drain well again.

Wash the lemon with hot water, dry, finely grate the zest, and squeeze the juice. Peel and finely dice the onion and garlic. Sauté both in 2 tbsp olive oil until translucent. Stir in the spinach and cream cheese. Season with about 2 tbsp lemon juice, 1 tsp lemon zest, salt, and pepper. Set aside.

In a frying pan, heat a little olive oil. Using the batter, cook 6 to 8 thin pancakes one at a time over medium heat.

Fill the pancakes with the spinach mixture. Sprinkle with chilli flakes, remaining lemon zest, and sesame seeds.

PREPARATION TIME: 45 minutes plus 15 minutes resting

WINTER VEGETABLE RICE DISH

A variety of vegetables and – most importantly – fragrant spices like ginger, curry, fennel, and mustard seeds turn this simple rice dish into comfort food par excellence. Top it off with plenty of creamy yogurt and fruity mango chutney, of course!

SERVES 4

VEGAN

250 g Brussels sprouts
1 medium leek
200 g carrots
25 g fresh ginger
3 tbsp vegetable oil
1½ tsp brown mustard seeds
1½ tsp fennel seeds
3 tsp hot curry powder
1 tsp ground turmeric
400 g basmati rice
2–3 tbsp lime juice
Salt
Freshly ground black pepper

TO SERVE

2 tbsp coriander leaves
400 g plant-based yogurt (e.g. coconut yogurt)
4–6 tbsp mango chutney (from a jar)

Clean and peel the vegetables as needed. Quarter the Brussels sprouts, cut the leek into thin rings, and slice the carrots thinly. Peel and finely chop the ginger.

In a pot, heat 1 tbsp vegetable oil and briefly sauté the ginger. Stir in the mustard seeds, fennel seeds, curry powder, and turmeric. Add the rice and pour in 800 ml water. Bring to a boil and simmer for 10–12 minutes, stirring occasionally, until done.

Meanwhile, heat 2 tbsp vegetable oil in a wok or large frying pan. Sauté the vegetables over high heat for 5–8 minutes until well browned. Season with lime juice, salt, and pepper.

Chop the coriander and stir it into the yogurt.

Combine the vegetables and rice. Serve on plates topped with the yogurt and mango chutney.

PREPARATION TIME: 60 minutes

POTATO-SPELT PATTIES WITH CREAMY CUCUMBER SALAD

These hearty patties are perfect for using up leftover boiled potatoes. They're also delicious cold, so you can easily pack them in a lunchbox.

SERVES 4

PATTIES
500 g potatoes (e.g. floury type)
Salt
150 g coarse spelt flakes
1 onion
1–2 garlic cloves
½ bunch parsley
2 eggs (size M)
Freshly ground black pepper
1–2 pinches freshly grated nutmeg
6–8 tbsp oil for frying

CREAMY CUCUMBER SALAD
2 salad cucumbers
Salt
150 g sour cream
3 tbsp white wine vinegar
1 pinch sugar
Freshly ground black pepper
4 tbsp rapeseed oil
½ bunch dill

Boil the potatoes in salted water for about 20 minutes. Drain, peel while still hot, and mash in a bowl.

Meanwhile, bring 300 ml water with ½ tsp salt to a boil. Add the spelt flakes and cook for 1 minute. Remove from heat and let sit for 5 minutes. Add the mixture to the mashed potatoes.

Finely dice the onion and garlic. Chop the parsley finely. Mix everything with the potato-spelt mixture and the eggs. Season generously with salt, pepper, and nutmeg. Let the mixture rest for 15 minutes.

For the salad: Thinly slice the cucumbers using a slicer or mandolin. Place in a bowl, sprinkle with salt, and let them release water for 10 minutes.

In the meantime, mix the sour cream, vinegar, sugar, pepper, and oil. Chop the dill finely and stir in. Squeeze the cucumbers well with your hands to remove excess water, then mix with the dressing. Set aside, covered.

Form 8-10 patties from the potato mixture with wet hands. Heat oil in a large pan and fry the patties over low to medium heat for 3–4 minutes per side until golden brown. Drain briefly on paper towels.

Serve the patties with the creamy cucumber salad.

PREPARATION TIME: 45 minutes plus 15 minutes resting

BREAD FROM THE WOOD-FIRED BAKERY

The brick oven looks as if it has always been here – or at least for a hundred years. In fact, it was installed only about fifteen years ago. Fifty tons of fireclay and bricks make up the wood-fired oven that forms the heart of the bakery. It is fired with large beech logs from the biodynamically farmed Gut Wulfsdorf estate.

Master baker Reinhold Hollerbach and his team begin work at 3:30 a.m., when the oven is fired up. It takes about an hour for the massive oven to reach baking temperature. At around 250°C, the first loaves are placed inside, then they bake gently as the heat gradually declines – this slow process results in an excellent aroma and a wonderfully crisp crust.

From seven base doughs, the master baker and his small team craft twenty varieties of bread and rolls. They work with rye sourdough, fermentation starters, and yeast. The rye, wheat, and spelt are grown on-site; additional ingredients are purchased and also come from Demeter-certified sources. No baking aids are added to the dough – instead, the dough is given ample time to develop flavour and volume. The atmosphere in the bakery is calm and focused. The workflows and movements seem well-rehearsed. Reinhold watches over everything, explains, demonstrates, and corrects when needed.

At the large worktable in the middle of the bakery, four or sometimes five bakers work simultaneously. They remove the dough from the large kneading machines, weigh, portion, shape it, and place the soft dough pieces with practiced hands into proofing baskets. A mildly sour, aromatic scent from the doughs hangs in the air, and in the next room, the grain mill hums steadily.

Now the moment has arrived – the oven has reached the right temperature. With practiced motions, a team member turns the well-risen doughs out of the proofing baskets onto a roughly three-metre-long floured wooden peel, which the master baker then slides through the oven hatch to the right position inside.

Loading the dough into the oven is sweaty work – heat streams out of the open hatch, and everything has to move quickly.

How long do the loaves stay in the oven? I ask the master baker.

The bread calls to me, he replies.

His internal clock tells him when it's time to open the oven hatch. He stabs a thermometer into a loaf to check the core temperature. Once baked, he removes the crispy loaves from the oven and places them on wooden racks to cool. They release a wonderful aroma that fills the bakery.

Then it's time for breakfast – naturally, with oven-fresh bread!

BREAD

FOCACCIA WITH ROSEMARY

This no-knead focaccia is incredibly simple to make. The dough rises for two days in the fridge and develops wonderful flavour and an airy texture during that long rest.

YIELDS: 1 BAKING DISH
VEGAN

- 1 tsp dry yeast (4 g)
- 1 tsp sugar
- 10 g salt
- 500 g wheat flour (Type 550)
- approx. 100 ml olive oil (for the pan and drizzling)
- Flaky sea salt for sprinkling
- 1 tbsp fresh rosemary leaves

About 48 hours before baking, stir 420 ml lukewarm water, yeast, sugar, and salt together. Add the flour and mix briefly with a wooden spoon until combined.

Transfer the dough to a large plastic container greased with olive oil. After 10 minutes, stretch and fold the dough several times until it becomes noticeably tighter. Repeat after another 10 minutes – the dough should now feel firm. Place it seam side down in the container and coat the surface with olive oil. Cover and refrigerate for about 48 hours.

Grease a baking dish (approx. 20 × 35 cm) with 2–3 tbsp olive oil. Place the dough into the dish. With oiled hands, fold one short side of the dough inward by one-third, then fold the opposite side over it. Rotate the dough 90 degrees and flip it over so the seam is on the bottom. Cover and let rest at room temperature (about 20 °C) for 2 hours. The dough should be very soft and full of air bubbles.

Preheat the oven to 220 °C/200 °C fan. Drizzle the dough with 3–4 tbsp olive oil and gently stretch it to fill the dish completely. Use oiled fingers to press deep dimples all over the dough.

Sprinkle with flaky sea salt and rosemary.

Bake in the preheated oven (lower rack) for about 20 minutes until golden brown.

PREPARATION TIME: 40 minutes + 48 hours resting + approx. 20 minutes baking

HEARTY TWISTED SPELT BREAD

Spelt has a pleasantly nutty flavour and is a nutritious regional alternative to rice. Sold as 'spelt rice' or 'spelt-like rice,' it refers to hulled, polished spelt grains that cook quickly.

MAKES 3 SMALL LOAVES

VEGAN

100 g 'spelt rice' (polished spelt grains)
Salt
250 g spelt flour (Type 630) + more for working
200 g whole spelt flour
¼ tsp dry yeast
1 tbsp lemon juice
330 ml cold water

The day before baking, cook the spelt rice in 200 ml water with a pinch of salt for about 20 minutes, covered. Drain in a sieve, let cool, and set aside.

In a bowl, combine both types of flour, the yeast, and 10 g salt. Stir in the lemon juice, cooked spelt rice, and cold water using a wooden spoon until a shaggy dough forms. Cover the bowl airtight and let the dough rise at room temperature for about 18 hours.

The next day, dust your work surface with flour and gently turn out the dough. Stretch and fold it three times at 10-minute intervals: first fold from right and left, then top and bottom. The dough will tighten each time. Form into a ball, cover, and let rest for 2 hours.

20 minutes before the rising time ends: Preheat the oven to 240 °C/220 °C fan. Place one baking tray in the middle of the oven and a second one on the bottom rack. Let both trays heat up for 20 minutes.

Divide the dough into three equal parts. Gently shape each into a log and twist each piece several times to form a spiral. Place on a sheet of parchment paper.

Remove the hot top tray from the oven and transfer the parchment with the twisted loaves onto it. Slide it back into the oven (middle rack). Pour a glass of water into the lower hot tray to create steam and close the door quickly.

Bake for 15 minutes. Then remove the steam tray, reduce the temperature to 200 °C/180 °C fan, and bake another 10-15 minutes until well browned and crispy.

PREPARATION TIME: 45 minutes plus approx. 20 hours resting and 25–30 minutes baking

FLUFFY BRIOCHE BURGER BUNS

When we have burgers at home, we love using these soft brioche buns to hold our veggie patties, fresh greens, and sauces.

MAKES 10 BUNS

- 500 g wheat flour (Type 550) + extra for working
- 50 g semolina (durum wheat)
- 100 ml milk
- 15 g fresh yeast
- 2 eggs (size M)
- 75 g soft butter
- 1 tsp salt
- 1 egg yolk + 1 tbsp milk for brushing
- 1 tbsp sesame seeds for sprinkling

For the pre-dough, place the flour and semolina in a mixing bowl and make a well in the centre. Warm the milk and 100 ml water until lukewarm, crumble in the yeast and dissolve it. Pour the mixture into the well and mix with a bit of flour from the edge to create a starter. Cover and let rise in a warm spot for 15 minutes.

Add the eggs, butter in small pieces, and salt. Knead with the dough hooks of a mixer for about 5 minutes until smooth. Shape the dough into a ball, dust lightly with flour, and return it to the bowl. Cover and let rise for another 30 minutes.

Preheat the oven to 200 °C/180 °C fan. Line a baking sheet with parchment paper.

Turn the dough out onto a lightly floured surface and divide into 10 equal pieces. Roll each piece into a smooth ball and place on the prepared sheet. Flatten each one slightly. Cover and let rise for another 30 minutes.

Whisk the egg yolk with the milk and brush the tops of the buns. Sprinkle with sesame seeds.

Bake in the preheated oven for about 20 minutes until golden. Remove and let cool.

PREPARATION TIME: 35 minutes plus 75 minutes rising and approx. 20 minutes baking

QUICK PUMPKIN SEED BREAD

It really couldn't be easier: Quickly mix the dough ingredients with water, pour the batter into a pan, place it in the cold oven, turn up the temperature, and bake. Take it out and let it cool. Then enjoy it slice by slice.

MAKES 1 LOAF (APPROX. 20 SLICES)
VEGAN

100 g pumpkin seeds + 3 tbsp pumpkin seeds
350 g whole spelt flour
250 g spelt flour (Type 630)
12 g salt
1½ packets dry yeast
2 tbsp vinegar (red or white wine vinegar)
2 tsp vegan margarine (for greasing the pan)
3 tbsp spelt flakes

Pour 100 ml boiling water over the 100 g pumpkin seeds and let soak for 2–3 hours. Drain off any excess water.

Mix both flours with the soaked pumpkin seeds, salt, and dry yeast in a large bowl. Combine 600 ml lukewarm water with the vinegar and pour into the bowl. Stir briefly with a wooden spoon to form a thick batter.

Grease a 30 cm loaf pan well with margarine. Roughly chop the 3 tbsp of pumpkin seeds and mix with the spelt flakes. Sprinkle half of this mixture into the bottom of the pan.

Pour the dough into the pan and smooth the top. Sprinkle the remaining pumpkin seed-flake mixture on top.

Place the pan into the cold oven. Then set the oven to 180 °C/160 °C fan, and bake the bread for about 45 minutes.

Remove from the oven, turn out of the pan, and let cool on a wire rack.

PREPARATION TIME: 10 minutes plus 3 hours soaking and approx. 45 minutes baking

ONE OVEN

HOT FROM THE OVEN

BAKED AND GRATINATED, STUFFED AND ROLLED

AUBERGINE POLENTA BAKE

Golden polenta forms the base of this Mediterranean-style bake with oven-roasted aubergine, fruity tomato sauce, and lots of cheese.

SERVES 4
VEGAN

FOR THE AUBERGINE AND SAUCE
2 aubergines (approx. 600 g)
approx. 4 tbsp olive oil
Salt, freshly ground black pepper
1 small onion
2 garlic cloves
½ bunch basil
400 g tinned chopped tomatoes
1 tsp sugar

FOR THE POLENTA
200 g polenta (cornmeal)
approx. 800 ml vegetable broth
1 small sprig rosemary

FOR TOPPING
approx. 30 g Parmesan cheese or non-dairy hard cheese
1 ball buffalo mozzarella (125 g) or non-dairy alternative

Preheat the oven to 240 °C/220 °C fan. Slice the aubergines lengthwise into approx. 1 cm thick slices. Arrange on a parchment-lined baking sheet, brush lightly with about 2 tbsp olive oil, and season with salt and pepper. Roast in the preheated oven for 12-15 minutes, until lightly browned and soft. Remove from the oven and reduce the heat to 200 °C/180 °C fan.

Meanwhile for the tomato sauce peel and finely chop the onion and garlic. Wash the basil, pat dry, finely chop the leaves and stems. Heat 1 tbsp olive oil in a saucepan, sauté the onion and garlic briefly, then add chopped basil stems, chopped tomatoes, sugar, and 100 ml water. Bring to a boil and simmer for 8–10 minutes to thicken. Stir in the chopped basil leaves and season with salt and pepper.

Prepare the polenta according to the packet instructions, using vegetable broth and the rosemary. Cook until creamy, remove the rosemary, and spread the polenta in a greased baking dish.

Finely grate the Parmesan and tear the mozzarella into small pieces.

Spread the tomato sauce over the polenta, layer the roasted aubergine slices on top, and finish with mozzarella and Parmesan.

Bake in the preheated oven (centre rack) for 25-30 minutes, until golden brown. Sprinkle with reserved basil leaves before serving.

PREPARATION TIME: 45 minutes plus 25-30 minutes baking

24-HOUR PIZZA MARGHERITA ALLA NAPOLETANA

My pizza dough rests for a full 24 hours, requiring only a tiny amount of yeast and developing wonderfully complex flavour. I use Italian soft wheat flour (Tipo 00), which gives the dough its elasticity and stretchiness. The topping is very simple – less is sometimes more. But feel free to get creative with a little garlic in the sauce; a few black olives or capers also work beautifully.

MAKES 3 PIZZAS

VEGAN

DOUGH

500 g soft wheat flour (Tipo 00 / pizza flour) + extra for working
½ g fresh yeast (just under pea-sized – don't use more!)
14 g salt
3–4 tbsp semolina (for shaping)
Olive oil (for greasing the container)

TOPPING

½ bunch basil
400 g tinned San Marzano tomatoes (peeled)
2 tbsp olive oil
Salt
Freshly ground black pepper
2 buffalo mozzarella (125 g each) or non-dairy alternative

PREPARATION (DAY 1, EVENING)

Place the flour in the bowl of a stand mixer. Add 300 ml cold water and mix briefly into a shaggy dough (or use a hand mixer with dough hooks if needed). Let the dough rest, covered, for 30 minutes (autolyse).

Dissolve the yeast in 1 tbsp cold water and add it to the dough. Knead at low speed for 5 minutes. Then add the salt and knead for another 10–15 minutes. The dough should come cleanly off the sides of the bowl.

Turn the dough out onto the work surface and stretch and fold it once. Transfer it to a large greased plastic container with a lid. Let rise at room temperature (approx. 20 °C) for about 18 hours.

PREPARATION (DAY 2)

Turn the dough out onto a lightly floured surface, divide into three equal portions, and shape each into a tight ball. Return them to the container and let rest another 6 hours at room temperature.

Preheat the oven to 250 °C/230 °C fan. If using a pizza stone, heat it for 30-45 minutes. Otherwise, preheat a baking sheet for 20 minutes.

Stretch each dough ball by hand (use the palms) into a circle about 30 cm in diameter on semolina-dusted parchment, keeping a puffy edge.

For the sauce: Wash and dry the basil. Tear the leaves, reserving a few whole ones. Crush the tomatoes with your hands in a bowl. Add chopped basil, olive oil, salt, and pepper. Tear the mozzarella into small pieces and pat dry.

Top each pizza with 2-3 tbsp tomato sauce (leave the edge bare), add mozzarella, and bake on the stone or hot tray for 10-15 minutes on the bottom rack until the crust is well browned and puffed.

Top with fresh basil leaves and serve.

PREPARATION TIME: 60 minutes plus over 24 hours rising and 10–15 minutes baking

PUMPKIN MILLET STRUDEL

Some say strudel dough is intimidating – difficult to roll out, tears easily, and takes too much time. Well, my dough isn't fussy, and if it does tear a bit while rolling out, it's no big deal! Thanks to the wholewheat flour content, this strudel dough is a bit thicker anyway – which suits the rustic charm of the strudel perfectly.

SERVES 6

VEGAN

STRUDEL DOUGH

150 g wheat flour (Type 405) + extra for working
100 g wholewheat flour
1 tsp salt
2 tbsp vegetable oil
1 tbsp white vinegar
125 ml lukewarm water

FILLING

600 g pumpkin flesh (weight after trimming)
250 g tomatoes
2 onions
2 garlic cloves
1 tbsp rosemary leaves
4 tbsp olive oil
Salt
Freshly ground black pepper
125 g millet
6–8 sun-dried tomatoes (in oil)
150 g feta or plant-based alternative
4 tbsp butter or non-dairy alternative

Make the dough by combining both flours, salt, oil, vinegar, and water. Mix with a hand mixer's dough hooks, then knead by hand into a smooth, soft dough. Cover and let rest at room temperature for 30 minutes.

Preheat the oven to 220 °C/200 °C fan. Line a baking sheet with parchment paper.

Dice the pumpkin into approx. 1.5 cm cubes. Roughly chop the tomatoes. Peel and finely chop the onions and garlic. Finely chop the rosemary.

Mix pumpkin, tomatoes, onion, garlic, rosemary, 2 tbsp olive oil, salt, and plenty of pepper. Spread on the prepared baking sheet and roast for 20 minutes. Remove and let cool slightly.

Meanwhile, rinse the millet in a fine sieve. Cook in 300 ml salted water for 8 minutes, then cover and let swell for 10 minutes. Drain if needed.

Finely chop the sun-dried tomatoes. Crumble the feta. Mix both with the millet and roasted vegetables. Season generously with salt and pepper.

To assemble the strudel, melt the butter. On a floured tea towel, roll the dough out thinly, then gently stretch it by hand into a 40×50 cm rectangle. Trim thick edges. Brush half the melted butter over the dough.

TO FINISH

1 tbsp white sesame seeds

1 tbsp black sesame seeds

Spread the filling over one half, leaving the edges clear. Using the towel, roll up the dough tightly. Tuck in the ends and transfer the strudel seam-side down onto the baking sheet.

Brush with the remaining butter and sprinkle with both sesame seeds.

Bake in the preheated oven (centre rack) for approx. 35 minutes until golden brown. Let rest for 5 minutes, then slice with a serrated knife.

PREPARATION TIME: 75 minutes plus 30 minutes resting and approx. 35 minutes baking

CRISPY CAULIFLOWER WINGS WITH SWEET-SPICY CHILLI SAUCE

I'd argue that even people who claim not to like cauliflower will happily gobble up this crispy treat. And if I want a break from chilli sauce, I whip up a yogurt dip packed with fresh garden herbs instead.

SERVES 4
VEGAN

CAULIFLOWER WINGS

1 large head cauliflower (approx. 1 kg)
200 ml plant-based milk (e.g. soy or oat)
75 g wheat or spelt flour
2 tsp Dijon mustard
Salt, pepper
75 g cornflakes
75 g panko or breadcrumbs
1 tsp sweet paprika
1 tsp cayenne pepper
4 tbsp olive oil (for brushing)

CHILLI SAUCE

3 tbsp coriander leaves
8 tbsp ketchup
1–2 tbsp sriracha (hot chilli sauce)
4 tbsp agave syrup
2 tsp wholegrain mustard
2 tbsp soy sauce
2 tbsp sesame seeds

Preheat the oven to 220 °C/200 °C fan. Line a baking sheet with parchment paper.

Break the cauliflower into florets, rinse, and drain thoroughly.

For the batter: Whisk together the plant milk, flour, and mustard in a bowl. Season with salt and pepper.

For the coating: Lightly crush the cornflakes with your hands into a second bowl. Add the panko, paprika, cayenne, and a pinch of salt; mix.

Dip the cauliflower florets first in the batter, allow excess to drip off, then roll them in the cornflake mixture to coat well.

Arrange the coated florets on the baking sheet. Dot or brush with olive oil. Bake for 20 minutes, then turn and bake another 20–25 minutes, until golden and crispy. Wedge a wooden spoon into the oven door during baking to allow steam to escape and enhance crispness.

For the sauce: Rinse, dry, and finely chop the coriander. Mix with all remaining ingredients to make the chilli sauce.

Drizzle the baked cauliflower with the sauce and sprinkle with the remaining coriander.

PREPARATION TIME: 30 minutes plus 40–45 minutes baking

RICE AND NUT ROAST

This savoury roast made from brown rice, nuts, mushrooms, and cheese is full of flavour. Sun-dried tomatoes, tomato paste, mustard, and soy sauce give it an extra umami punch. It makes 12 to 14 slices – more than enough for four hungry people. Leftovers are great pan-fried the next day.

SERVES 6–8

150 g brown rice
Salt
250 g mixed hazelnuts and walnuts
1 onion
1–2 garlic cloves
150 g mushrooms
8 sun-dried tomatoes (in oil)
1 bunch flat-leaf parsley
1 tbsp rosemary needles
150 g strong cheese
4 eggs (size M)
2 tbsp soy sauce
2 tbsp tomato paste
1 tbsp Dijon mustard
Freshly ground black pepper

Cook the rice according to packet directions in salted water. Drain well in a sieve and let cool.

Meanwhile, roast the nuts in a dry pan until golden brown and fragrant. Let them cool, then finely grind in a food processor.

Peel and finely dice the onion and garlic. Clean and slice the mushrooms thinly. Drain and finely chop the sun-dried tomatoes. Wash and finely chop the parsley and rosemary. Grate the cheese finely.

Preheat the oven to 180 °C/160 °C fan. Line a 25 cm loaf tin with parchment paper.

In a large bowl, whisk the eggs. Add the rice, ground nuts, chopped vegetables and herbs, grated cheese, soy sauce, tomato paste, and mustard. Mix well and season generously with salt and pepper.

Spoon the mixture into the prepared loaf tin and smooth the top.

Bake in the middle of the oven for about 50 minutes, until the roast is nicely browned.

Let rest for 10 minutes, then lift out using the parchment paper and slice with a sharp knife.

It goes well with a dip made from wholegrain mustard and sour cream.

PREPARATION TIME: 50 minutes plus approx. 50 minutes baking

STUFFED BEEFSTEAK TOMATOES

In summer, when large, fully ripe beefsteak tomatoes are in season, I love filling them with this Mediterranean grain mixture. A few slices of bread on the side, and you've got a perfect light summer meal.

SERVES 3–4

VEGAN

125 g whole oat grains
Salt
2 tbsp raisins
4 large beefsteak tomatoes (approx. 350 g each)
2 spring onions
1–2 garlic cloves
2 tbsp pitted green olives
½ bunch flat-leaf parsley
½ bunch basil
2 tbsp olive oil
1 tbsp lemon juice
2 tsp Ras el-Hanout
Freshly ground black pepper
250 ml vegetable broth

Place the oat grains in a pot, cover with water, and add a pinch of salt. Bring to a boil and cook for 20-25 minutes until tender. Add the raisins, bring to a boil again, then drain everything in a sieve and let it drain well.

Meanwhile, slice off a 'lid' from each tomato and carefully scoop out the insides with a spoon. Set the tomato water aside and finely chop the pulp.

Clean and finely slice the spring onions. Peel and finely chop the garlic. Chop the olives. Rinse the herbs, dry them, and finely chop the leaves and tender stems.

Preheat the oven to 200 °C/180 °C fan.

Combine the chopped tomato pulp, spring onions, garlic, olives, and herbs with the cooked oats and raisins. Add the olive oil, lemon juice, and Ras el-Hanout. Season with salt and pepper. Mix well.

Fill the tomatoes with the mixture and place in a baking dish. Replace the tomato 'lids'. Pour the vegetable broth and reserved tomato water into the dish.

Bake in the preheated oven for about 20 minutes.

PREPARATION TIME: 30 minutes plus approx. 20 minutes baking

PORTOBELLO MUSHROOMS WITH FREEKEH FILLING AND YOGURT SAUCE

Freekeh is made from green, roasted durum wheat and has a bold, smoky flavour. Popular in Levantine cuisine, it's still somewhat unfamiliar here. You can substitute it with green spelt, spelt, or wheat if needed.

SERVES 4

MUSHROOMS
150 g freekeh
Salt
4 portobello mushrooms (large, approx. 150 g each)
3 tbsp olive oil
Freshly ground black pepper
4 tbsp hazelnuts
200 g feta cheese
½ bunch dill
½ bunch parsley
1 tsp fennel seeds
1 egg (size M)
150 g crème fraîche
1 tsp chilli flakes

YOGURT SAUCE
1 garlic clove
350 g crème fraiche
1 tsp finely grated zest of an untreated lemon
Salt
Freshly ground black pepper

TO GARNISH
½ pomegranate
2 tsp sumac

For the filling: Cook the freekeh in lightly salted water for about 25 minutes, covered, until tender but still slightly firm to the bite. Drain and let cool.

Preheat the oven to 200 °C/180 °C fan. Clean the portobellos and twist out the stems. Lay the mushrooms gill-side up in a baking dish, brush with 1 tbsp olive oil, and season with salt and pepper.

Finely chop the mushroom stems and hazelnuts. Crumble the feta. Wash and finely chop the dill and parsley. Lightly crush the fennel seeds in a mortar.

Mix all these with the freekeh, egg, crème fraîche, and chilli flakes. Season to taste with salt. Spoon the filling into the mushrooms.

Bake for about 20 minutes in the preheated oven.

Meanwhile, prepare the yogurt sauce: Press the garlic into the crème fraîche, stir in the lemon zest, and season with salt and pepper.

Remove the seeds from the pomegranate.

To serve, spread the yogurt sauce on a platter, place the mushrooms on top, and sprinkle with pomegranate seeds and sumac.

PREPARATION TIME: 40 minutes plus 30 minutes cooking and approx. 20 minutes baking

RUSTIC BEETROOT CROSTATA

The tender wholemeal crust encases a juicy filling of oven-roasted beetroot, caramelised onions, and goat cheese – it simply has to taste delicious!

SERVES 4

FILLING

600 g beetroot
6 tbsp olive oil
3 tbsp balsamic vinegar
1 heaped tbsp flavourful honey
2 tbsp lemon juice
Salt
Freshly ground black pepper
4 onions
2 tsp summer savory or thyme leaves
100 g soft goat cheese (e.g. chèvre log)

SHORTCRUST PASTRY

225 g wholemeal flour (e.g. kamut, wheat, or spelt) + extra for working
25 g sesame seeds + 1 tbsp for sprinkling
½ tsp salt
125 g cold butter
1 egg (size M)
2 tbsp breadcrumbs
2 tbsp milk (for brushing)

Preheat the oven to 200 °C/180 °C fan. Peel the beetroot and slice into rounds approx. 1 cm thick. In a baking dish, toss beetroot slices with 3 tbsp olive oil, balsamic vinegar, honey, lemon juice, salt, and pepper. Roast for 30 minutes, until just tender. Remove and let cool.

Meanwhile for the dough, mix the flour, sesame seeds, and salt in a bowl. Add the cold butter in pieces and rub into coarse crumbs using your hands or a hand mixer. Add the egg and 2-3 tbsp cold water, knead quickly into a smooth dough. Wrap and refrigerate for 30 minutes.

Peel and finely dice the onions. Sauté in 2 tbsp olive oil over medium heat for about 10 minutes until soft. Stir in the herbs and season with salt and pepper. Slice the goat cheese.

Roll out the dough on a floured surface into a circle (about 35 cm in diameter) and transfer to a parchment-lined baking sheet.

Sprinkle the dough with the breadcrumbs, then layer on the sautéed onions, goat cheese slices, and roasted beetroot, leaving a 5 cm border all around. Fold the edge of the dough loosely over the filling.

Brush the crust with milk and sprinkle with 1 tbsp sesame seeds.

Bake on the lower rack of the oven for 30–35 minutes, until golden and crisp.

PREPARATION TIME: 60 minutes plus 30–35 minutes baking

CRISPY GREEN SPELT BALLS WITH HUMMUS AND TAHINI SAUCE

I always make a double batch of these veggie balls – they taste just as delicious cold as they do hot. And with hummus and tahini yogurt sauce, everyone's happy.

SERVES 4

VEGAN

GREEN SPELT BALLS

1 small red pepper
1 small onion
1 garlic clove
4 tbsp olive oil
200 g cracked green spelt
600 ml vegetable broth
½ bunch flat-leaf parsley
approx. 50 g breadcrumbs
1 tsp ground cumin
Salt
Freshly ground black pepper

HUMMUS

250 g tin or jar chickpeas
1–2 garlic cloves
3 tbsp tahini (sesame paste)
3 tbsp good olive oil
1–2 tbsp lemon juice
Salt
1 tsp ground cumin

To make the green spelt balls, core and finely dice the pepper. Peel and finely dice the onion and garlic.

Heat 2 tbsp olive oil in a saucepan and sauté the pepper, onion, and garlic for 1–2 minutes. Add the cracked green spelt and vegetable broth, bring to a boil, then simmer over low heat for about 15 minutes, stirring occasionally.

Turn off the heat and let the mixture swell for another 10 minutes. Remove from heat and allow to cool until lukewarm.

Preheat the oven to 200 °C/180 °C fan. Line a baking sheet with parchment paper.

Rinse and dry the parsley, finely chop the leaves and stems. Mix the parsley, breadcrumbs, and cumin into the green spelt mixture. Knead into a formable mass and season with salt and pepper.

With moistened hands, form balls about 4 cm in diameter and place them on the baking sheet. Lightly brush with the remaining 2 tbsp olive oil and bake in the preheated oven for 20-25 minutes, until crispy and golden brown.

TAHINI YOGURT SAUCE

2 heaped tbsp tahini

150 g plant-based yogurt

1 tbsp lemon juice

Salt

Freshly ground black pepper

ALSO

4 tbsp pomegranate syrup for drizzling

4 tbsp pomegranate seeds and herb leaves for sprinkling

Meanwhile, prepare the hummus: Rinse the chickpeas in a sieve and drain. Peel and roughly chop the garlic. Place chickpeas, garlic, tahini, olive oil, and lemon juice in a mixing container and purée with an immersion blender. Add warm water, one spoonful at a time, until the dip is thick and creamy. Season with salt and cumin.

For the sauce mix the tahini with the yogurt, 2-3 tbsp water, and lemon juice until smooth. Season with salt and pepper.

Remove the balls from the oven and serve with the hummus. Drizzle with the tahini yogurt sauce and pomegranate syrup, then sprinkle with pomegranate seeds and herbs.

PREPARATION TIME: 75 minutes + 20–25 minutes baking

STUFFED AUBERGINES WITH QUINOA AND FETA

Before their trip to the oven, the aubergines take a brief bath in salted water, which softens them and allows them to soak up more of the delicious filling. Once filled and baking, everything melds together into a Mediterranean delight. Lovely alongside a creamy tahini yogurt dip.

SERVES 4

4 small aubergines (250-300 g each)
Salt
5 tbsp olive oil
100 g quinoa
2 onions
2–3 garlic cloves
1 small yellow pepper
1 handful parsley leaves
2 tbsp mint leaves
2 tbsp pitted black olives
3 tbsp tomato paste
1 tsp chilli flakes
2 tsp cumin seeds
1½–2 tsp Ras el-Hanout
75 g feta

Peel about five lengthwise strips of skin from each aubergine using a vegetable peeler and set them aside. Cut out a 3-4 cm wide wedge lengthwise from each aubergine and also set aside. Score the interior of the aubergines in a crisscross pattern with a small knife, cutting down to the skin – this helps them cook faster. Submerge the aubergines in heavily salted water (2 litres water with 4 tbsp salt) for 30 minutes, placing a plate on top to keep them submerged.

Preheat the oven to 200 °C /180 °C fan. Remove the aubergines from the water and drain well. Place them in a large baking dish, drizzle with 2 tbsp olive oil, cover tightly, and pre-bake in the hot oven for 30 minutes.

Meanwhile, rinse the quinoa thoroughly under running water, then cook in salted water for 12–15 minutes. Drain well and let cool in a bowl.

Peel and finely dice the onions and garlic. Deseed the pepper and cut into small cubes. Finely dice the reserved aubergine wedges and skin strips. Rinse and finely chop the parsley and mint. Roughly chop the olives.

Heat 3 tbsp olive oil in a pan and sauté the onions, pepper, and aubergine cubes for about 5 minutes, stirring. Stir in the garlic and tomato paste, pour in 200 ml water, and season with chilli flakes, cumin, Ras el-Hanout, and a little salt. Bring to a boil and simmer gently for about 3 minutes.

Add half of this vegetable mixture to the quinoa. Crumble in the feta, add the herbs and olives, and mix everything well.

Remove the pre-baked aubergines from the oven and gently press the flesh aside to make room for filling. Fill the cavities with the quinoa mixture. Spread the reserved vegetable mixture around the aubergines in the dish and pour in enough water to come about finger-height up the side. Cover with a sheet of parchment paper and return to the oven to bake for about 45 minutes.

PREPARATION TIME: 45 minutes plus 30 minutes soaking and approx. 75 minutes baking

BUCKWHEAT GALETTES WITH CAMEMBERT AND APPLE

Who doesn't love crispy Breton crêpes – or rather galettes, as the savoury buckwheat-based versions are called? They're popular in neighbouring Normandy too. My favourite topping couldn't be more typical for this northern French region known for its lush apple orchards and creamy white rind cheese.

SERVES 4

BATTER

25 g butter, plus 4 tsp butter for cooking
250 ml milk
60 g buckwheat flour
60 g wheat flour (Type 405)
2 eggs (size M)
Salt

TOPPING

3 medium tart apples
2 tbsp butter
2 tbsp brown sugar
5 tbsp apple juice or water
200 g Camembert
2–3 tsp thyme or marjoram leaves

For the galettes: Melt 25 g butter and let it cool to lukewarm. Combine the milk, both flours, eggs, melted butter, and ½ tsp salt into a smooth batter. Let rest for 15 minutes.

Meanwhile, prepare the topping. Quarter and core the apples, then slice them into thin wedges. Melt the butter with the sugar in a pan. Add the apple wedges and sauté over medium heat for about 5 minutes, until soft and golden brown, shaking the pan occasionally. Pour in the apple juice or water and allow to reduce briefly.

Preheat the oven to 180 °C/160 °C fan.

In a non-stick pan, heat 1 tsp butter. Pour in a quarter of the batter and fry over medium heat for about 2 minutes per side, until golden brown and thin. Remove and repeat to make three more galettes.

Place all galettes side-by-side on a parchment-lined baking tray. Slice the Camembert thinly and arrange it with the apple slices in the centre of each galette. Fold the edges loosely over the filling.

Bake on the middle rack of the preheated oven for 5–10 minutes, until the cheese melts.

Remove from the oven and sprinkle with the herbs.

PREPARATION TIME: 30 minutes plus 15 minutes resting and 5–10 minutes baking

A FEAST FOR THE EYES AND FOR BEES: BUCKWHEAT CULTIVATION

From afar, the field with its white blossoms stands out; the plants sway gently in the summer wind, and the closer we get, the louder the buzzing and humming in the field becomes. 'Walking through a blooming buckwheat field is like a fountain of youth! There is so much life in these fields – I've never experienced anything like it on any other field,' says Kay Hansen, who grows buckwheat in Germany.

The organic farmer came across buckwheat cultivation more or less by chance. One of his fields was heavily waterlogged in late spring, and he considered which grain he could still sow at such a late time. He tried buckwheat – and stuck with it. Sandy soils are particularly well suited for buckwheat cultivation, as the plants can thrive in nutrient-poor soils.

Buckwheat originally comes from East Asia, but from the Middle Ages until the 19th century, it was cultivated throughout Central Europe. Back then, it was considered a poor man's food, as it could grow even on poor, barren land. With the growing popularity of the potato and the intensification of agriculture, buckwheat lost its importance and almost completely disappeared from local fields. The name suggests that buckwheat is a type of grain. But botanically, buckwheat is a member of the knotweed family and not a true grain – it is classified as a pseudo-cereal. Its fruit is a three-sided nut that resembles a beech nut in shape but is much smaller.

In recent years, buckwheat cultivation has seen a resurgence. There are various reasons for this: One is the growing awareness of health – buckwheat is gluten-free, rich in vitamins, minerals, and the beneficial

plant nutrient rutin. Additionally, demand for locally sourced organic food has significantly increased. For farmers, buckwheat is appealing to grow because, due to its late sowing time, it does not displace other crops in the rotation. Buckwheat is only sown in mid-May, when the risk of frost is low. 'It doesn't like frost! The plants turn brown at just minus 0.5 degrees Celsius,' says Kay.

Buckwheat grows quickly, and after a short time, the plants shade much of the soil, preventing weeds from spreading significantly. In early July, it begins to bloom in white and delicate pink, filling the fields with bees – it buzzes and hums everywhere.

Harvesting, however, is complicated. The ideal harvest time falls between mid and late September, is short, and difficult to pinpoint. This is because buckwheat ripens very unevenly – among the many brown kernels, there are always some green ones. While the lower parts of the plant bear ripe, brown kernels, new blossoms are still forming at the upper end of the reddish stalk. After harvesting, the small kernels must first go into a drying facility. Another challenge is the dehulling process, as the buckwheat husk is very hard and prone to breaking. However, dehulling in mills specifically designed for this purpose is essential, since even prolonged cooking does not soften the husk of these small brown seeds.

It's no surprise, then, that buckwheat remains a niche product compared to higher-yielding grains – but what a delicious one it is!

BULGUR CAKE WITH TOMATO-FIG SALAD

Bulgur is made from wheat, just like couscous. For this, wheat grains are cooked, dried, freed from the bran, and then cut into fine, medium, or coarse pieces depending on the size.

SERVES 4–6
VEGAN

BULGUR CAKE

250 g medium-fine bulgur
Salt
400 g cooked potatoes (e.g. from the day before)
3 spring onions
½ bunch coriander
½ bunch parsley
6 tbsp olive oil
approx. 2 tbsp flour
1½ tsp ground cumin
1 generous pinch freshly grated nutmeg
½ tsp ground cinnamon
½ tsp ground turmeric
Freshly ground black pepper

TOMATO SALAD

250 g cherry tomatoes
2–3 ripe figs
4 tbsp lemon juice
1 tsp agave syrup
½ tsp ground cinnamon
Salt, freshly ground black pepper
3 tbsp olive oil
1 handful coriander leaves

Preheat the oven to 200 °C/180 °C fan. Grease a baking dish (approx. 18×25 cm) with olive oil.

Cook the bulgur in boiling salted water for 2 minutes, then remove the pot from the heat and let it soak. Drain through a fine sieve, press out excess water with a spoon, and let cool.

Mash or finely crush the potatoes and mix with the bulgur in a bowl.

Trim and finely slice the spring onions. Finely chop the herbs. Add spring onions, herbs, 3 tbsp olive oil, 2 tbsp flour, the spices, about 1½ tsp salt, and plenty of pepper to the potatoes and bulgur. Knead thoroughly and season boldly. The mixture should be elastic but not too soft; if needed, knead in another tbsp of flour.

Spread the bulgur mixture into the baking dish. Score a deep diamond pattern into the top with a knife and drizzle with the remaining olive oil. Bake in the centre of the oven for about 45 minutes.

Meanwhile, quarter the cherry tomatoes and slice the figs into thin wedges. For the dressing, whisk lemon juice, agave syrup, cinnamon, a bit of salt, pepper, and olive oil. Rinse and dry the coriander leaves and coarsely chop them. Combine the tomatoes, figs, and coriander with the dressing and let sit for a few minutes.

Cut the cake into pieces and serve with the salad.

PREPARATION TIME: 50 minutes plus approx. 45 minutes baking

LEEK QUICHE

Emmer, like einkorn, is considered an ancient grain. It thrives even in nutrient-poor soil and is cultivated almost exclusively through organic farming. Emmer flour has a stronger flavour than wheat flour and stands out for its high mineral and protein content.

SERVES 4–6

SHORTCRUST PASTRY

250 g wholegrain emmer flour (or wheat or spelt wholegrain flour) + extra for dusting
150 g cold butter
1 egg (size M)
Salt
Butter for the pan
2 tbsp breadcrumbs (for sprinkling)

TOPPING

750 g leeks
1 onion
1–2 garlic cloves
2 tbsp vegetable oil
300 g sour cream
3 eggs (size M)
1 tbsp flour
1 tbsp thyme leaves
Salt, freshly ground black pepper
Freshly grated nutmeg
100 g blue cheese

Place the flour in a mixing bowl. Add the butter in small cubes, the egg, a good ½ tsp salt, and 2–3 tbsp cold water. Knead into a smooth dough. Wrap in foil and chill for 30 minutes.

Meanwhile, clean the leeks thoroughly and slice thinly. Peel and finely dice the onion and garlic. Heat the oil in a wide pot and sauté the onion and garlic. Add the leeks, 4–5 tbsp water, and cook covered for 6–8 minutes, stirring occasionally so it doesn't burn. Remove from heat.

First stir in the sour cream, then the eggs, flour, and thyme. Season well with salt, pepper, and nutmeg. Crumble the blue cheese and mix in.

Preheat the oven to 200 °C/180 °C fan. Grease a 26-cm spring-form pan. Roll out the dough slightly larger than the pan and press it in, forming a small rim. Prick the base with a fork and sprinkle with the breadcrumbs.

Spread the filling over the dough. Bake on the lower rack for about 45 minutes, until golden brown. Let rest for 5 minutes before slicing.

PREPARATION TIME: 60 minutes plus 30 minutes chilling and approx. 45 minutes baking

DRESDEN

CAKE

MEDITERRANEAN PEACH CROSTATA WITH THYME

The dough for this Mediterranean treat becomes especially tender and flaky when not kneaded too thoroughly – small visible flecks of butter are explicitly desired!

MAKES 8 SLICES

VEGAN

DOUGH

250 g einkorn wholemeal flour (or wheat or spelt wholemeal flour) + extra for working
70 g brown sugar
2 pinches salt
125 g cold butter or non-dairy alternative
75 g crème fraîche or non-dairy alternative
2 tbsp breadcrumbs

FILLING

800 g ripe, juicy peaches
50 g brown sugar
1 tbsp thyme leaves
1 tbsp cornflour
2 tbsp pine nuts
2 tbsp milk or plant-based alternative and 2 tbsp brown sugar (for the crust)
1–2 tbsp peach or apricot jam

For the dough, rub the flour, sugar, salt, cold butter in small flakes, and crème fraîche into coarse crumbs. Add 2–3 tbsp ice-cold water and quickly knead everything into a dough. The dough should not be over-kneaded – small, pea-sized butter pieces should still be visible. Wrap in foil and chill for 60 minutes.

Meanwhile, halve and pit the peaches, then slice the halves into wedges about 1 cm wide. Mix the peach wedges in a bowl with the sugar, thyme, and cornflour. Let it sit briefly to release some juice.

Preheat the oven to 200 °C/180 °C fan. Line a baking sheet with parchment paper.

Roll out the dough on a lightly floured surface into a circle about 32 cm in diameter, and place on the baking sheet. Sprinkle the breadcrumbs over the base. Spread the peaches over the dough, leaving a 5 cm border all around. Fold the edge of the dough loosely over the peaches. Sprinkle the pine nuts over the peaches.

Brush the crust with milk and sprinkle with the brown sugar.

Bake the crostata on the lower rack of the preheated oven for 30–35 minutes, until the crust is nicely browned. Remove from the oven and brush the peaches with the slightly warmed and smoothed jam.

PREPARATION TIME: 40 minutes plus 60 minutes chilling and 30–35 minutes baking

CRISPY RHUBARB CAKE WITH SPELT CRUMBLE

The crumble dough forms both the base for the rhubarb and a thick topping of streusel. This easy and quick cake isn't just delicious with rhubarb – it also works wonderfully with apple slices, blackberries, or blueberries. A spoonful of whipped cream or crème fraîche is always a good idea.

MAKES 12 SLICES
VEGAN

CRUMBLE DOUGH

300 g spelt flour (Type 630)
150 g ground almonds or hazelnuts
Seeds of 1 vanilla pod
1 tsp grated zest of an untreated lemon
1 tsp ground cinnamon
160 g brown sugar
1 pinch of salt
300 g cold butter or non-dairy alternative
Butter or non-dairy alternative and flour for the pan

TOPPING

approx. 700 g rhubarb
2 tbsp brown sugar

Preheat the oven to 180 °C/160 °C fan. Grease a 26-cm spring-form pan and dust with flour.

For the crumble dough: Mix the flour, nuts, vanilla seeds, lemon zest, cinnamon, sugar, and salt in a bowl. Add the butter in small pieces and rub everything together into crumbles.

Press about two-thirds of the dough into the prepared pan to form a base and a short rim, pressing the crumbles down well. Pre-bake in the hot oven for about 15 minutes, then remove and allow to cool slightly.

Meanwhile, trim and cut the rhubarb into pieces about 3 cm long. Distribute the rhubarb pieces evenly over the pre-baked crust. Sprinkle with brown sugar. Top with the remaining crumbles.

Bake for another 30–35 minutes until golden and crisp.

Remove the cake from the oven and let it cool in the pan on a wire rack for about 30 minutes, then carefully remove from the pan.

PREPARATION TIME: 40 minutes plus 45–50 minutes baking

MOIST APRICOT CRUMBLE WITH ALMONDS AND GINGER

As soon as the first French apricots hit the market, I can't help myself. Alongside jars of apricot jam, at least one crumble made with these red-blushed fruits must be baked each season – ideally served with a big spoonful of crème fraîche.

SERVES 4
VEGAN

CRUMBLE
- 75 g butter or non-dairy alternative, plus extra for greasing
- 40 g unblanched almonds
- 15 g fresh ginger
- 60 g whole spelt flour
- 75 g + 25 g brown sugar
- 60 g coarse spelt flakes
- ½ tsp ground cinnamon
- Seeds of ½ vanilla pod
- 1 tsp finely grated zest of an untreated lemon
- 1 generous pinch of salt

FRUIT
- 750 g apricots
- 3 tbsp lemon juice

Melt the butter for the crumble and allow it to cool slightly. Roughly chop the almonds. Peel and finely chop the ginger.

In a mixing bowl, combine the lukewarm butter with almonds, ginger, flour, 75 g sugar, spelt flakes, cinnamon, vanilla seeds, lemon zest, and salt. Rub into coarse crumbs. Cover and chill for 30 minutes – this makes them especially crispy.

Preheat the oven to 200 °C/180 °C fan.

Halve and pit the apricots. Grease a large gratin dish. Lay the apricots inside, drizzle with lemon juice, and sprinkle with the remaining 25 g sugar. Let it sit briefly so the fruit releases some juice.

Distribute the crumble evenly over the apricots. Bake in the preheated oven for about 30 minutes, until the topping is golden and crispy.

PREPARATION TIME: 25 minutes plus approx. 30 minutes baking

SWEET CARDAMOM-HONEY ROLLS

These fluffy yeast rolls hold a juicy filling of butter, honey, and cardamom – absolutely finger-licking good.

MAKES 12 ROLLS

YEAST DOUGH

240 ml milk
25 g fresh yeast
60 g sugar
550 g wheat flour (Type 550) + extra for working
2 eggs (size M)
75 g cold butter
10 g salt
Butter for greasing the pan

FILLING

12–15 green cardamom pods
175 g soft butter
100 g mild honey (e.g. sunflower honey)
75 g brown sugar
35 g cornflour
1 tsp ground cinnamon
2 tsp finely grated zest of an untreated orange

ALSO

2 tsp powdered sugar for dusting

The evening before: Warm the milk until lukewarm. Crumble in the yeast, add 1 tsp sugar, stir, and let stand for 15 minutes.

Mix the flour with the yeast mixture, remaining sugar, eggs, cold butter in flakes, and salt. Knead with the dough hooks of a hand mixer into a smooth, elastic dough. Shape the dough into a ball on a lightly floured surface, return it to the bowl, cover, and refrigerate overnight (at least 12 hours).

The next day: Turn the dough out onto a floured surface, cover, and let rise for 60 minutes.

For the filling: Crack the cardamom pods and remove the black seeds. With a hand mixer, combine the soft butter, honey, sugar, cornflour, cinnamon, orange zest, and cardamom seeds until smooth.

Grease a baking dish (approx. 20×30 cm). Roll out the yeast dough on a lightly floured surface into a rectangle approx. 30×45 cm. Spread the filling evenly across the dough. Roll up the dough from the long side, then slice into 12 pieces. Place the rolls cut-side up in the baking dish. Cover and let rise for another 60 minutes.

Preheat the oven to 200 °C/180 °C fan. Bake the rolls in the preheated oven (lower-middle rack) for about 30 minutes until golden brown, covering if necessary partway through.

Remove from the oven, let cool slightly, and dust with powdered sugar.

PREPARATION TIME: 45 minutes plus several hours resting and approx. 30 minutes baking

SEASONAL CALENDAR

VEGETABLES

	JAN	FEB	MAR	APR	MAY	JUN	JUL	AUG	SEP	OCT	NOV	DEC
ARTICHOKES	○	○	○	○	○	●	●	●	●	●	○	○
ASPARAGUS	○	○	○	○	●	●	○	○	○	○	○	○
AUBERGINES	○	○	○	○	○	○	○	●	●	⁘	○	○
BEANS	○	○	○	○	○	○	●	●	●	●	○	○
BEETROOT	⁘	⁘	⁘	⁘	○	○	●	●	●	●	⁘	⁘
BLACK KALE	●	●	○	○	○	○	○	○	○	●	●	●
BLACK SALSIFY	●	●	○	○	○	○	○	○	○	●	●	●
BROCCOLI	○	○	○	○	○	●	●	●	●	●	○	○
BRUSSELS SPROUTS	●	○	○	○	○	○	○	○	○	●	●	●
CARROTS	⁘	⁘	⁘	⁘	⁘	●	●	●	●	●	⁘	⁘
CAULIFLOWER	○	○	○	○	○	●	●	●	●	●	○	○
CELERIAC	⁘	⁘	⁘	⁘	⁘	⁘	⁘	●	●	●	●	⁘
CELERY STALKS	○	○	○	○	○	○	●	●	●	●	○	○
COURGETTES	○	○	○	○	○	●	●	●	●	●	○	○
CUCUMBERS	○	○	○	○	○	○	●	●	○	○	○	○
DAIKON (WHITE RADISH)	○	○	○	○	●	●	●	●	●	●	○	○
FAVA (BROAD) BEANS	○	○	○	○	○	○	●	●	○	○	○	○
FENNEL	○	○	○	○	○	○	●	●	●	●	○	○
GARLIC	⁘	⁘	⁘	⁘	⁘	○	●	●	●	●	⁘	⁘
JERUSALEM ARTICHOKES	⁘	⁘	⁘	⁘	○	○	○	○	●	●	●	●
KALE	●	●	○	○	○	○	○	○	○	○	●	●

● HIGH SEASON ○ NOT IN SEASON ⁘ STORAGE

	JAN	FEB	MAR	APR	MAY	JUN	JUL	AUG	SEP	OCT	NOV	DEC
KOHLRABI	○	○	○	○	●	●	●	●	●	●	○	○
LEEKS	●	○	○	○	○	●	●	●	●	●	●	●
ONIONS	⁘	⁘	⁘	⁘	⁘	⁘	●	●	●	●	⁘	⁘
PAK CHOI	○	○	○	○	○	●	●	●	●	○	○	○
PARSLEY ROOT	⁘	⁘	⁘	⁘	⁘	○	○	○	●	●	●	⁘
PARSNIPS	⁘	⁘	○	○	○	○	○	○	●	●	●	●
PEAS	○	○	○	○	○	●	●	●	○	○	○	○
PEPPERS	○	○	○	○	○	○	●	●	●	●	○	○
POTATOES	⁘	⁘	⁘	⁘	⁘	●	●	●	●	●	⁘	⁘
PUMPKIN	⁘	⁘	○	○	○	○	○	○	●	●	●	⁘
RADISHES	○	○	○	○	○	○	●	●	●	●	○	○
RAMSON (WILD GARLIC)	○	○	●	●	○	○	○	○	○	○	○	○
RED CABBAGE	⁘	⁘	⁘	⁘	⁘	○	○	●	●	●	●	⁘
RHUBARB	○	○	○	●	●	●	○	○	○	○	○	○
ROCKET	○	○	○	○	●	●	●	●	●	●	○	○
SAVOY CABBAGE	○	○	○	○	●	●	●	●	●	●	●	⁘
SNOW PEAS	○	○	○	○	●	●	○	○	○	○	○	○
SPINACH	○	○	●	●	●	●	○	○	●	●	●	○
SWEDE	⁘	⁘	○	○	○	○	○	●	●	●	●	●
SWEET POTATOES	⁘	⁘	○	○	○	○	○	○	○	●	●	⁘
SWEETCORN	○	○	○	○	○	○	○	●	●	●	○	○
SWISS CHARD	○	○	○	○	○	●	●	●	●	●	○	○
TOMATOES	○	○	○	○	○	○	●	●	●	●	○	○
WHITE & POINTED CABBAGE	⁘	⁘	⁘	⁘	⁘	●	⁘	⁘	●	●	●	⁘

FRUITS

	JAN	FEB	MAR	APR	MAY	JUN	JUL	AUG	SEP	OCT	NOV	DEC
APPLES	⁘	⁘	⁘	⁘	⁘	○	○	●	●	●	⁘	⁘
APRICOTS	○	○	○	○	○	○	●	●	○	○	○	○
BLACK CURRANTS	○	○	○	○	○	●	●	●	○	○	○	○
BLACKBERRIES	○	○	○	○	○	○	○	●	●	○	○	○
BLUEBERRIES	○	○	○	○	○	○	●	●	○	○	○	○
DAMSONS	○	○	○	○	○	○	○	●	●	○	○	○
FIGS	○	○	○	○	○	○	○	●	●	○	○	○
GOOSEBERRIES	○	○	○	○	○	●	●	●	●	○	○	○
GRAPES	○	○	○	○	○	○	○	●	●	●	○	○
MELONS	○	○	○	○	○	○	○	●	●	○	○	○
MIRABELLES	○	○	○	○	○	○	○	●	●	○	○	○
NECTARINES	○	○	○	○	○	○	●	●	○	○	○	○
PEACHES	○	○	○	○	○	○	●	●	○	○	○	○
PEARS	⁘	○	○	○	○	○	○	●	●	⁘	⁘	⁘
PLUMS	○	○	○	○	○	○	○	●	●	○	○	○
QUINCES	○	○	○	○	○	○	○	○	●	●	●	○
RASPBERRIES	○	○	○	○	○	●	●	●	●	○	○	○
RED CURRANTS	○	○	○	○	○	●	●	●	○	○	○	○
SOUR CHERRIES	○	○	○	○	○	○	●	●	○	○	○	○
STRAWBERRIES	○	○	○	○	●	●	●	●	●	○	○	○
SWEET CHERRIES	○	○	○	○	○	●	●	●	○	○	○	○

RECIPE INDEX

ACKNOWLEDGEMENTS

Saskia Lackner and Tillmann Spies from Bohlsen Mill

We bombarded you with questions for hours, and you patiently and knowledgeably explained the workings of the mill. We could truly feel the spirit of the old mill and your passion for the milling craft, and we've come to appreciate the value and quality of regional organic products even more.
www.bohlsener-muehle.de

Reinhold Hollerbach and the entire baking team of the Demeter wood-fired bakery at Gut Wulfsdorf

You opened the bakery doors for us in the early morning – it felt like the middle of the night – and despite the busy pace, you let us take all our photos, answered our many questions, and shared with us a delicious breakfast of oven-fresh bread.
www.gutwulfsdorf.de

Kay Hansen and Conrad Torkler

In summer, you led us to the white-blooming buckwheat fields; in autumn, we were able to join you for the buckwheat threshing. Along the way, we learned a lot about organic grain cultivation in general – and buckwheat farming in particular – thanks to you.

Maria Antonelli from Jill's Pasta

You welcomed us into your little pasta haven and showed us how, with great dedication, you turn *semola*, water, and salt into tagliatelle, tagliolini, and ravioli – all while giving us a mini masterclass in Neapolitan cooking. *Grazie mille!*
www.jillspasta.de

Janet

Wherever there's a need during a photo shoot, you're there – whether with your sharp photographer's eye or your kitchen skills. You make sure everything runs smoothly and are a calming presence on chaotic shoot days.

Annette and Florian

You both love working in the garden, making compost teas and herbal brews, saving tomatoes from blight, lettuces from slugs, and artichokes from aphids. You're our test eaters for everything cooked, baked, braised, or roasted in the studio kitchen – and you do that job brilliantly too!

ANNE-KATRIN WEBER lives with her family in Hamburg. She is a cook and nutritionist, a freelance author of numerous award-winning cookbooks and baking books, and a sought-after food stylist for print and advertising.

Anne-Katrin Weber loves cooking with vegetables and usually starts developing her recipes with the "greens" – which she adores not only on the plate, but also in the garden. She grew up with her grandmother's wood-fired bread and only years later realised that *Schwarzbrot* – the sourdough bread with the black crust from her Swabian homeland – has absolutely nothing in common with a Hamburg-style *Schwarzbrot*. To this day, nothing beats a good slice of buttered bread for this passionate bread lover.

www.annekatrinweber.de

WOLFGANG SCHARDT is one of Germany's most successful food photographers. His visual style is clean, modern, and marked by a refined sense of aesthetics. He works in his studio for publishers and advertising clients.

For this book, he more often left the studio behind, crisscrossing Hamburg and the northern German countryside with Anne-Katrin. He returned with countless documentary-style photos that capture grain processing, wood-fired baking, pasta making, and buckwheat cultivation – and a few delicious samples in tow.

Just as his work is mostly centered on culinary topics, Wolfgang is also a dedicated foodie in his private life. He loves good cuisine and wine, and is an avid cook himself – especially when it comes to vegetables and fruits from his own garden.

www.wolfgangschardt.com

ANNE-KATRIN WEBER and **WOLFGANG SCHARDT** are united not only by a long-standing friendship, but also by their shared culinary magazine, where this photographer-author duo expresses their passion for creative, delicious vegetable-based cuisine.

Published in 2025 by
Grub Street
4 Rainham Close
London
SW11 6SS

Email: food@grubstreet.co.uk
Web: www.grubstreet.co.uk
Twitter/X: @grub_street
Facebook: Grub Street Publishing
Instagram: grubstreetpublishinguk

Published originally in German as *Greens & Grains*
Photography: Wolfgang Schardt

A CIP catalogue record for this book is available from the British Library.

ISBN 978-1-911714-30-9

Printed and bound by Finidr in Czechia